THE MODERN HOUSE BUS

THE COUNTRYMAN PRESS
A division of W. W. Norton & Company
Independent Publishers Since 1923

Kimberley Mok

THE MODERN HOUSE BUS

Mobile Tiny House Inspirations

Manufacturing by Versa Press
Book design by Jackie Shao
Production manager: Devon Zahn

The Countryman Press
www.countrymanpress.com

A division of W. W. Norton & Company, Inc.
500 Fifth Avenue, New York, NY 10110
www.wwnorton.com

978-1-68268-249-4

10 9 8 7 6 5 4 3 2 1

Contents

8   Introduction

23   **The House Buses**
24   We Got Schooled
38   Natural State Nomads
52   Developing Apps and Homeschooling on a Bus
64   Adventure or Bust
76   Where We Roam
90   Building a Bus Cottage and Minibus RV
110   Big Bertha
124   Living Bus Life to the Fullest
134   The Professor and Her Champion
146   The Midwest Wanderers
160   The Yetibus
174   By the Grace of the Queen of Peace

193   **Choosing and Renovating a House Bus**
196   Getting Started
202   Design, Layout, and Construction
224   Tips for a Healthier, More Efficient Home
226   Registration, Licensing, and Insurance
228   Places to Park

230   Afterword

231   Resources
232   Bibliography
233   Contributors
236   Photo Credits
237   Index
240   About the Author

"THE JOURNEY
IS MY HOME."

MURIEL RUKEYSER

There are many kinds of buses: bright yellow school buses, city buses that one might take on the way to work, coach buses that zip between cities, and shuttle buses that are smaller and more nimble on the road. But have you ever thought of a bus as a place to call home? Some people may think it odd or eccentric to live in a renovated bus. Yet a growing number of ordinary folks are choosing to do just that. Some choose the "bus life" because they are looking for an alternative to the rat race, with its high-pressure jobs, huge mortgage debts, sky-high rents, and outsize lifestyle costs. Some aim to reduce their living expenses so that they can have more time and financial freedom to do what they truly love. Others are looking to travel the country in a recreational vehicle customized for their needs. Regardless, each of them is defining their own version of the American Dream.

But many of these individuals, couples, and families with kids aren't the stereotypical bohemians you might expect to live on a bus. Rather, they are tech entrepreneurs, business owners, professors, interior designers, web developers, photographers, filmmakers, blue-collar folks—people from all walks of life—who have opted to revamp these vehicles into beautiful homes. By leveraging technologies like broadband wireless Internet and cheap solar power, they are able to do their work, run their businesses, and stay connected while on the road.

This book is a visual tour of the thoughtfully and creatively designed homes on wheels that these enterprising bus homeowners have made for themselves. As you'll discover, some of these homes stay in place, while others are mobile and allow their owners to travel from place to place with comfort and flexibility. These fascinating stories reveal how this emerging trend of modern and stylishly built bus homes comes from the intersection of America's robust RV culture and the emerging "tiny house" and digital nomadism movements. Those who follow this trend exhibit how these portable, self-designed homes are permitting them to live their lives on their own terms. Along the way, you'll get a look at the basics behind the process of converting a bus, including tips from the bus owners themselves. Consider this book a call to think outside the box, a challenge to ask yourself what you need to live a fulfilled and meaningful life.

The Tiny House Movement (a.k.a. Mortgage-Free Housing)

A growing number of people are looking for alternatives to the status quo. For most, the notion of "home" is a house or an apartment with exterior walls, a bedroom or two or more, a kitchen and a bathroom, and perhaps a balcony or a big lawn and backyard. In addition to a conventional home, "success" and the "good life" for many include a shiny new car, a closet stuffed full of clothes, and a purse or pocket full of all the latest gadgets.

However, having all these trappings of success often comes at a high price. It can mean exchanging our free time for grinding commutes, working long hours at uninspiring jobs, paying down a decades-long mortgage or making the monthly rent for an apartment, and repaying any personal debt we may have

MIGHT WE BE HAPPIER WITH FEWER THINGS AND A SMALLER HOME?

accrued. It's a tradeoff that leads many of us to wonder whether we are truly happy giving up most of our free time in a never-ending pursuit of bigger, shinier things. Might we be happier with fewer things and a smaller home, especially if that means doing away with a mortgage and having more freedom and time to do the things that matter most to us? Now what if this smaller home was on wheels?

This idea of a mortgage-free, tiny home on wheels isn't as crazy as it sounds. In fact, these so-called "tiny homes" have been gaining popularity in recent years, thanks to the housing market crash and global recession of the late 2000s. When the housing bubble burst, many people were forced to default on their enormous debts—as many as 9.3 million American families lost their homes to foreclosure. The apparent breakdown of the cherished American ideal of "anything is possible if you work hard" caused many to become disillusioned and to look for alternatives to an unfair and broken system. There had to be a better way.

It was around this time, after the housing bubble collapsed, that interest in mortgage-free tiny homes exploded. These tiny but robust homes are usually sized at 400 square feet or less, and come in a variety of styles. The smaller footprint of tiny homes means that it costs less to

Two examples of tiny houses—one is the "typical" tiny house with a gabled roof (left), the other is built with a more modern aesthetic (right).

outfit them with high-quality materials. Many are also built on wheeled trailer bases to make them portable, meaning that if you move, you get to keep your home. Many of these tiny dwellings are built by the homeowners themselves, and they are often great examples of stunning design and clever multifunctionality. Not surprisingly, there's an environmentally friendly aspect to tiny houses too. They require less materials, produce less construction waste, and are generally more energy-efficient in the long run to maintain: their low energy requirements mean they can rely on solar power or other alternative forms of energy.

But the biggest and most compelling difference between tiny and conventional homes may be the price tag. Tiny houses typically cost a fraction of a conventional home to construct, usually anywhere from $15,000 and up for self-built structures, and from $40,000 to $100,000 for professionally built tiny homes. Even at these prices they contain many of the usual attributes of a "regular" house: comfortable sitting areas, well-equipped kitchens, bedrooms, and bathrooms. The idea of being able to build and own your own home outright, without needing to borrow money, appeals to many, especially to those who were affected by the housing market crash.

HOME SHOULD BE A VEHICLE FOR HELPING YOU LIVE THE LIFE YOU WANT.

In addition, tiny houses are symbols of a more sustainable, simpler lifestyle where "less is more." They stand in stark contrast to the excesses associated with large suburban houses, including the high maintenance costs and heavy mortgage debts. While tiny houses may run counter to the culturally ingrained obsession for "bigger is better," there are commonsense reasons and practical benefits to sizing things down. In 2015 the average size of the American home reached an all-time high of 2,687 square feet, an increase of 1,000 square feet from 1973. During the same time period, the average household in the United States has actually become smaller, resulting in more square footage of living space per person. Many of the spaces in these large homes, such as dining rooms and formal living rooms, are rarely used. All this unused space costs a lot of money to heat and cool. Plus, these empty spaces further encourage needless consumerism, becoming places to store extra "stuff" that's rarely used, much less needed. The ultimate catch of having all this stuff is that even the process of acquiring and maintaining it takes precious time and energy that could be better spent on more fulfilling activities.

The problem of wasted time and space is compounded by the big mortgages that are usually attached to these larger homes—and often require decades to pay off. Americans hold about $10 trillion in mortgage debt, with the average mortgage loan pegged at $309,200 in 2017. That would mean the average borrower can expect to pay $1,494 in monthly principal and interest for the next 30 years, not including property taxes and premiums on homeowner's insurance. That's a lot of debt to bear. So in the larger scheme of things there are financial benefits to living in smaller homes with fewer possessions. For starters, one may not need to take out a loan to build a smaller house. Moreover, it is much cheaper to maintain this smaller space than a 3,000-square-foot (or larger) home.

Because many tiny homes are built on wheels and are generally smaller than the minimum size requirements of many local zoning regulations, they are often built under the radar and exist in a legal gray zone. But that is slowly changing. The International Code Council (ICC) is now taking preliminary steps to have tiny houses included in future versions of the international residential building code. Tiny homes are also gaining mainstream traction, as evidenced by official tiny house residential developments and dedicated communities that are cropping up across North America and beyond.

In light of these factors, smaller homes are beginning to make a lot of sense. The dawning realization that smaller may actually be better is gaining ground, fueling interest in all kinds of smaller homes, be they tiny homes on wheels, renovated shipping containers, prefabricated units, and yes, converted vehicles. But the essence of the tiny house ethos is that no matter what your home looks like, it should be a vehicle for helping you to live the life you want, rather than a burden that shackles you with debt and locks you into a lifestyle of overconsumption. It's a trade-off for more freedom: by living more simply with a smaller footprint, you can save more money and have more free time to do the things that you want to do.

It's little wonder that tiny homes are now being touted as one possible alternative for more flexible, affordable, and sustainable housing. But they also represent a redefinition of what happiness and a "good life" looks like.

A Tiny History of Camping Culture, RVs, and Bus Conversions

Emerging out of today's intense interest in tiny homes is a renewed enthusiasm for portable homes on wheels of all kinds. In particular, there has been an uptick in popularity of automotive vehicles such as vans, school buses, and motorcoaches, which are being converted into modern tiny homes. Bus-to-motorhome conversions typically cost even less than buying a conventional RV or building a run-of-the-mill tiny house, and they are a great choice for those who want to be as mobile as possible. Many of these modern house bus conversions adapt refined design cues from the tiny house

Top: The most well-known early motorhome was owned by the Conklin family of Long Island, New York, 1915.

Bottom: A housecar named Harriet at the Tin Can Tourists convention, 1929.

Page 16: Ken Kesey and the Merry Pranksters' famous bus, nicknamed Further, at a festival near Seattle, Washington, 1994. This was its second incarnation.

movement, and they are being conceived and constructed with the same goals of cost-effectiveness, sustainability, flexibility, and mobility in mind.

Of course, bus conversions are nothing new. They have been around since before the introduction of the first affordable car and the popularization of "auto-camping" back in the early 1900s. As James B. Twitchell recounts in his history of modern RV culture, *Winnebago Nation,* the concept of escaping the grind of city life and camping in the great outdoors for amusement finds its roots in the 1850s during the Romantic period, with wealthy Victorian estate owners who decorated "gypsy wagons" for weekend camping and hunting trips.

In America the love for the quintessential "road trip" begins with the Ford Model T, the first affordable car for the masses. As Warren Belasco posits in *Americans on The Road: From Autocamp to Motel, 1910–1945,* the automobile gave people a way to rebel en masse against the rigid schedules and routes of rail travel, allowing them to explore the country in a wider scope.

During that time, captains of industry, including Henry Ford, Thomas Edison, and Harvey Firestone, took to the road in caravans of modified "housecars" to encourage the public to take "auto-camping" vacations by automobile. It was around this time that early motorists and their families began to roam the country at their own pace and according to their own whims, often in tricked-out vehicles. These customized housecars evolved in complexity and stature, eventually leading to one of the first motorhome conversions in America, commissioned by Roland R. Conklin, president of the American Motor Bus Company. Conklin and his family converted a bus into an English-style manor, nicknamed the "Superior Truck" or more whimsically, the "Gyspy Van," complete with an upstairs deck for dining and dancing, full kitchen, furniture, and

enough space for a family of six and staff of two to live comfortably.

Today's domestic tourism industry, characterized by a national network of pit stops and quirky tourist attractions, got its start when these early travelers and their dollars were welcomed by local communities in balmy places such as Florida. Almost overnight, tourist campgrounds and trailer parks sprung up to host these temporary, mobile communities of auto travelers. These so-called Tin Can Tourists—named either for their penchant for eating newly invented canned goods while on the road or for their affection for Ford's "Tin Lizzie" Model T—effectively pioneered early camper travel.

As Kate Trant outlines in *Home Away From Home: The World of Camper Vans and Motorhomes*, Americans' love affair with the road trip deepened with the introduction of the first commercially produced motorhome in the 1940s. This was further encouraged by the gradual development of a national network of

interstate highways during the middle of the 20th century. These elements helped lay the foundation for the camping vacation as we now recognize it, both in the United States and abroad, in addition to sowing the seeds for the modern nomadic culture of road-bound travelers who journey from coast to coast in RVs, trailers, camper vans, and modified vehicles of all kinds.

Old Bus, New Tricks

The popular stereotype of the bus-dwelling bohemian isn't completely without cause. One might trace the association between bus conversions and hippie counterculture through American novelist and LSD advocate Ken Kesey, author of the seminal novel *One Flew Over the Cuckoo's Nest*. Kesey and a group of his friends, calling themselves the Merry Pranksters, made a cross-country trip in a converted bus from San Francisco to New York to publicize Kesey's second book in 1964. Their journey was a

transcendental attempt to make art out of the everyday and to experience the American road trip, while literally tripping on psychedelics. The vibrantly painted bus, nicknamed Further (or Furthur, depending on the mood) carried Kesey and his companions as they spread the message of enlightenment and the ideals of freedom that were at the heart of psychedelic culture.

The popular association between bus conversions and the hippie counterculture was emphasized further when a group of more than 200 people, led by activist and hippie icon Stephen Gaskin, set out from San Francisco in a caravan of 40 converted buses, trucks, and vans to look for affordable land to form an intentional community. The travelers eventually settled in Tennessee in 1971, founding the community now known as The Farm. Many of the buses from the pilgrimage were then converted into full-time residences. Though it has evolved over the years, The Farm exists to this day, endeavoring to live up to its ideals of mutual cooperation and care, and is also known as the birthplace of the modern natural childbirth movement.

These ideas were relatively radical in the sixties. Yet over time, many of the movements and ideals of that era—free speech, gender and racial equality, peace, nuclear disarmament, spiritual enlightenment, responsible environmental stewardship—have evolved and become so integrated in our collective consciousness that we mostly take them for granted.

The lasting impact of these ideological seeds can be seen behind many current trends, such as mainstream interest in eco-friendly lifestyles, the growing acceptance of the ideas of minimalism, and simple living.

The Rise of the Digital Nomad and the Freelance Economy

While bus dwelling may have been viewed in the past as a radical act, best suited for those who had dropped out of society, this stereotype is shifting toward something quite unexpected. New technologies are drastically changing how many people live and work across all social strata, allowing a growing number of people to travel and work wherever they please.

The Internet is the biggest enabler of these radical shifts in work and living habits during the last decade. For starters, portable and wireless technologies, videoconferencing, and a host of cloud-based applications and other innovative platforms are permitting many to work remotely. Only an Internet connection or a cell phone signal are needed. Almost everything that has traditionally required a stationary, brick-and-mortar office setting can now be done on the road.

These are the driving factors behind the burgeoning, global "digital nomad" movement. People might choose to become a member at a coworking space (a shared office space for freelancers), or to travel and take up residence in different parts of the world, maintaining "location independence" without the need for a daily commute. Of course, it's also possible to live the digital nomad lifestyle while traveling in a recreational vehicle.

Yet another factor in this shift is the rise of the so-called freelance economy. The global job market is changing rapidly thanks to new technologies. Right now, 53 million Americans are freelancers (making up 34 percent of the workforce), either as independent contractors, moonlighters, temporary workers, or self-employed business owners. It's estimated that by 2020, more than 40 percent of the US workforce, or 60 million people, will be freelancing.

One survey found that 33 percent of freelancers were able to travel more because they were freed from the constraints of a traditional office job. Just as it dismantled the illusion of one's house being a secure investment, the Great Recession of the late 2000s broke down the illusion of the secure office job, prompting many to cope with an uncertain job market by becoming freelancers or starting their own businesses.

Buses vs. Vans vs. Tiny Homes vs. RVs

Some may ask: Why not just purchase a ready-made RV instead of going to all the trouble of building out a bus?

While ready-made RVs require less effort than DIY conversions, and certainly look flashier, there are some distinct advantages to converting a bus or motorcoach into a custom motorhome. For starters, RVs can be costly to buy, especially if they are new. Furthermore, made with lightweight, flimsy materials and intended for occasional use, RVs are nowhere near as solidly built or as capable on rough terrain as, say, a school bus. School buses are constructed to an almost tanklike degree of durability because they must carry and protect throngs of schoolchildren day in and day out. Moreover, they must reliably operate in all weather conditions and be able to handle uneven and sometimes unpaved rural roads. It almost goes without saying that school buses are better equipped than RVs for off-road driving.

School buses are generally outfitted with robust engines that are capable of clocking up to half a million miles, or even more. With regular maintenance and care they will run strong even after years of service. Depending on the type of bus, they are also cheaper to buy—retired school buses in good working condition can be purchased for a few thousand dollars, due to plentiful supply. In addition, a school bus offers a rich variety of customization options, as compared to a mass-produced RV.

Renovating a bus from scratch can also be significantly less expensive than building a tiny house from the ground up, especially if you do the work yourself. For those looking to move around frequently, buses are a good choice because they are much more mobile than a tiny house built on a wheeled trailer base. Moving a tiny house frequently is a hassle, as it often requires careful planning and a powerful truck to pull it. What's more, renting or buying such a truck can represent a substantial extra cost.

For owners of vans that have been converted into full-time residences, buses are a step up in terms of space and possibilities. For those raising kids, living the van life may be too cramped, but a bus can offer them just the right amount of space for maintaining an affordable mobile lifestyle.

The Environmental Impact of Bus Life
Beyond the financial benefits, there are other compelling reasons to choose a smaller home, such as reducing one's overall environmental footprint. Everything that we do has some kind of impact on the environment, whether it's the waste we generate, or living in a big suburban home that's far from our place of work, or driving a fuel-inefficient car. Living in a bus conversion requires its own set of considerations in this ecological equation. Perhaps the most obvious is that a bus is a rather hefty vehicle that requires a lot of fuel—most buses only get a few miles to the gallon.

NEW TECHNOLOGIES ARE DRASTICALLY CHANGING HOW MANY PEOPLE LIVE, ALLOWING A GROWING NUMBER TO TRAVEL AND WORK WHEREVER THEY PLEASE.

But how much of an environmental impact bus dwelling will have ultimately depends on one's habits. One may live in a fuel-guzzling metal beast, but if it's not conveniently hooked up to an established water service or electrical grid, or garbage isn't being taken away on a regular basis, then one is bound to reduce one's water and electrical usage, and reduce the amount of waste too. When limits are placed on our consumption levels, or when we are directly confronted with the outputs of our habits—that is, we go without the services that keep them "out of sight, out of mind"—we tend to adapt by making things simpler. These shifts in lifestyle habits add up and can ultimately lessen overall environmental impacts.

For instance, a study on sustainability at RV parks done by Harvard University Extension School found that on average, a Class C motorhome might only expend 13 to 15 kilowatt-hours of electricity in one night. In comparison, according to the US Energy Information Administration, the average daily electricity consumption for a US residential utility customer in 2016 was around 30 kilowatt-hours.

Even the gasoline consumption of those who lead such alternative nomadic lifestyles might be less than that of those who live more conventionally. For instance, even though full-time RVers do drive around and consume fuel, on the whole they might actually drive less than the 13,500 miles that the average American accumulates annually during the daily commute to work, school, running errands, and so on. One's environmental footprint might be further lessened by converting a bus to run on biodiesel or recycled waste vegetable oil (WVO), which is usually taken from fast food restaurants.

The Do-It-Yourself Ethos

Yet another factor behind the emerging trends in tiny house living and vehicle conversion is the immense satisfaction (and cost savings) that people get from building their own homes with their own hands. These enterprising individuals might not have previous construction experience, but with the wealth of knowledge that's easily available online and elsewhere, it's now possible to learn how to build many things yourself. Being a DIY

"maker" has become a badge of honor to be worn proudly. And the possibilities for hands-on creativity will only increase as this popular movement around tinkering, crafting, and hobbies grows.

In addition, doing a renovation yourself can mean higher-quality results, because you, the homeowner, will be less likely than a professional builder to cut corners in order to pad profits. You

HOME IS WHERE WE REMAIN CENTERED.

will be much more likely to take your time to create and realize a more personalized design, and to try to do things right from beginning to end. And should something break down, you'll have the skills and know-how to troubleshoot and fix the problem yourself.

It's little wonder that people are drawn to the idea of building their own

homes, whether on wheels or otherwise. It can be a challenging but ultimately empowering experience.

Communities of Shared Lifestyles

Despite the untethered nature of nomadic subcultures, such as those of the full-time RVer or the globe-trekking digital nomad, loose communities of these populations do exist. The urge to connect, to belong, and to identify with a greater group or common purpose is a universal human desire, no matter the living situation.

Communities in the RV world have a large range. They include informal alliances that spring up between visitors camping at a state park, a themed RV resort, or popular wintering locations such as those found in Florida or in Quartzsite, Arizona. They also include more formal allegiances such as the Escapees, a national organization of more than 200,000 RV owners, many of them full-timers. Belonging to these groups usually affords members a sense of belonging and fellowship: "They know each other not by shared experience, but by shared lifestyle," writes Twitchell in *Winnebago Nation.*

In the tiny house world, that sense of community is found through official tiny house developments that are emerging as various municipalities legalize tiny homes. That's in addition to innumerable unofficial communal arrangements across the country where one or a few tiny houses might share a backyard behind a larger house. Tiny house festivals are popping up all over North America, bringing tiny house homeowners and the curious public together in one place. Events like these effectively foment discussion on the state of housing policy and create a kind of cultural cross-pollination.

Bus conversion enthusiasts might find themselves somewhere in the overlap of these two worlds. Many bus converters embrace the same ideals about debt-free housing and creative DIY ethos as those in the tiny house movement, but similar to RVs, buses are also relatively more mobile. The result is a growing community of bus homeowners who find themselves forging connections with each other—whether online in "skoolie" (or school bus conversion) forums and on social media or in person. No matter the venue, they are able to engage each other with a diverse spectrum of experiences and perspectives, filtered through a shared lifestyle.

Home Is Where You Park It

A new cultural trend has emerged from the convergence of these elements. Bus conversions and other small-home solutions are appealing to a wide range of people, whether they are looking for more financial freedom or more travel. Tiny homes on wheels can also be an affordable option for those who want to build a high-quality, customized recreational vehicle for less, or who have previously converted smaller vehicles and are looking to upgrade.

In addition, as we become freed from the constraints of geographical location, many of us will also likely work while we satisfy the itch to wander, thanks to new technologies that allow us to work from anywhere. Our ideas of "home" will evolve. Rather than a building located at a fixed address, we might begin to see that the notion of home is a way of understanding and structuring the space around and within us. Home is where we remain centered and feel "at home" within ourselves. It becomes a space of belonging and state of mind that we carry with us on the inside, no matter where we go, no matter where we live, even if it's a bus.

THE HOUSE BUSES

WE GOT SCHOOLED

After years of working long hours in stressful jobs, Austin, Texas–based couple Justine Meccio and Ryan Ayers felt they were missing out on something. The pair, who document their bus travels on the blog *We Got Schooled*, decided to make some changes. They began saving more money and living more simply, and eventually decided that they wanted to avoid the costs and debt associated with a conventionally constructed home.

They were intrigued by the idea of living in a self-built, affordable, and ultra-mobile tiny home. With the aim of traveling to see more of the world, they ultimately chose to convert an old school bus. It took about 20 months of working through nights, weekends, and vacations to complete the build, and they were grateful for the help of Justine's father on trickier things like installing the electrical wiring. Later during this period, both saved enough money to quit their jobs and focus on the bus conversion full-time.

Tips:

- Make sure to take the time to refine the design using a real-life, full-size mock-up on the bus
- A cheaper version of professional automotive paint can be adapted from urethane-based paint for marine and industrial use, with hardeners mixed in

---

Features:

- Solar power system used for lights, refrigerator, water pump, fan, sound system, charging devices, consisting of a 300-watt solar panel system from Renogy; a 1,500-watt continuous/3,000-watt peak performance inverter from Cen-Tech; and two 6-volt deep-cycle batteries from Trojan
- Magic Chef electric refrigerator
- SHURFlo water pump

The couple used digital drawing and design tools to develop a preliminary layout. They used masking tape and cardboard later on in the process to create a full-size mock-up on the empty bus itself, which they used to further refine their design. Thanks to this tactic, they were able to simplify the design and create a much more open living area.

In total, the couple spent about $15,000 on the entire project, including $5,000 to purchase and repair the bus. Thanks to these efforts, their living expenses have been significantly reduced. Now that they live on the bus, the income brought in by Ryan's work as a freelance computer programmer, and from Justine's freelance photography contracts, make their lifestyle financially possible.

Since moving in and embarking on their travels in their renovated bus home, the couple and their two cats have adjusted well to the quirks of living in 200 square feet of space.

"We're much more mindful of our water and energy usage now, and use less electricity than we did in our former home," says Justine. "Not having much space keeps us from casually buying things at the rate we used to when we lived in a house. Having a smaller fridge and limited pantry space has resulted in less household food waste and actually improved our diet—we cook fresh meals every day. Likewise, we no longer spend hours watching television, playing video games, or just leaving household appliances running in the background."

From the ouside, the bus is a turquoise beauty. Inside, it features a spacious living room, kitchen, bathroom with shower, bedroom, and roof deck. The main living space feels larger thanks to the simplified design. Bright colors and a light-toned material palette give the space an airy sense of openness, as does the deliberate absence of overhead shelving.

A set of bookcases is made from stacked milk crates and finished with pine boards. Wooden rods are inserted into the milk crate openings to keep books secure while the bus is in motion.

Right and opposite: Plants help make the small space feel more vibrant, and custom-made planters prevent the succulents from sliding around. Justine and Ryan made sure to fill their space with meaningful keepsakes and quirky objects to make it feel like a home, rather than a vehicle.

Page 32: The compact kitchen includes a small sink and a Camp Chef propane camping oven, surrounded by decorative metal sheeting. Pots, pans, and dishes are stored in oak-faced drawers, and a rack for hanging utensils allows for easy access. The glass-tile countertop has a small lip around it to stop things from slipping off.

Page 33: Located between the kitchen and the bedroom, the bathroom can be closed off from the rest of the bus with a sliding door. An additional curtain is used to separate the bathroom from the bedroom. A standard Aqua-Magic RV flush toilet has been installed, which connects to a 20-gallon black water tank below. The bus is also equipped with a 17-gallon gray water tank, and a 40-gallon freshwater tank that typically lasts about 7 to 10 days before needing to be refilled. The shower uses fiberglass reinforced panels (FRP) and an RV-style shower pan to create a waterproof space. A controlled-flow RV showerhead helps to minimize water use. The bus uses a tankless water heater to produce hot water on demand.

A queen-size bed fills most of the bedroom, but there's still enough space for built-in shelving at the foot of the bed and above. A laundry bag hangs in one corner. The couple kept the bus's original metal ceiling so that they could use heavy-duty magnets to add extra storage hooks and decorative elements. The back door still functions as an emergency exit.

The sleekly painted exterior was achieved with a urethane-based paint for marine and industrial applications from Sherwin-Williams, which was then hand-mixed with a hardener and applied in two coats with an airless sprayer.

The bus also features a roof deck. An array of rooftop solar panels power most of the appliances and Internet connection, which allows the couple to work remotely while on the road. Another great feature is the bus's custom-built, portable crane (page 36). It is used for lowering bulky items like a kayak and bicycles down from the roof. To get around when the bus is parked, they use their bicycles.

NATURAL STATE
NOMADS

With the rise of remote work, no longer do people need to be squeezed into office cubicles to be considered gainfully employed. Now, thanks to innovative software platforms and ultra-portable devices, entrepreneurs, software programmers, filmmakers, writers, and creatives of all stripes can work remotely from anywhere they want, as long as there's an Internet connection.

The idea of being able to work while traveling appealed to Arkansas couple Zack Andrews and Annie King. A few years ago they were living the conventional life: punching in at regular office jobs and paying down a mortgage on a house. But they also loved to travel, and they would rent a car to visit new places whenever they had time off. However, they invariably found that this kind of travel was too rushed and didn't allow them to take their time to see or do everything on their list.

When Zack heard about bus conversions through a coworker who lived in an RV full-time, the couple began to research more about school bus conversions. Zack eventually landed a job as a web developer, which allowed him to work remotely. Seizing on this opportunity, Annie decided to quit her corporate job so that the couple could finally take the plunge together.

"DOING IT YOURSELF HAS THE ADDED BENEFIT THAT IF ANYTHING GOES WRONG, YOU KNOW HOW TO FIX IT."

They sold their house and purchased a 2001 Thomas Saf-T-Liner handicap-accessible bus for $9,000. They put about $20,000 into the renovations, doing much of the construction work themselves. They learned the ropes of installing electrical, plumbing, and solar power systems with the help of online tutorials and forums, and with a bit of help from Zack's father.

Their bus, which they have nicknamed Stormy, exudes a Zen-like presence inside, thanks to the open design, a contrasting palette of light and dark surfaces, and clean, minimal lines. The design maximizes every inch to reduce unused space. Clever storage options are everywhere, from inside the armrests of the custom-made couch to the refrigerator that's actually a converted chest freezer.

The bus relies on solar power for all the appliances and gadgets, and it carries its own 150-gallon water tank. The couple can go completely off the grid whenever they wish, and they can stay comfortably (and even work) in remote areas for up to two weeks. Zack, who has always been a tinkerer, undertook the challenging task of figuring out and installing the electrical system himself—a big DIY achievement. "Doing it yourself also has the added benefit that if anything goes wrong, you know how to fix it," he says.

In addition to allowing them to simultaneously work and travel, their nomadic life has brought the two into contact with people from all walks of life, as well as other nomads. Since heading out on their travels, Zack and Annie have attended skoolie meet-ups and festivals, where bus homeowners congregate and share stories and tips.

"Everyone starts out as strangers at the gatherings, but it really feels like you are with family by the time everyone leaves," says Zack. "You immediately have a common bond over going through the conversion process, as most have done their own builds, as well as bonding over the nuances of living a nomadic life. In general, the skoolie community is very helpful because chances are that one of us has been in the same situation and through the same dilemma. Everyone tries to help out and give advice whenever they can."

Tips:

- To maximize space, incorporate function into "dead spaces"—like incorporating storage or a cup holder into a couch
- Consider a DIY conversion of a chest freezer into a super-insulated and super-efficient refrigerator, using online tutorials
- To save money, take the time to collect off-cuts and salvaged materials from secondhand material or construction stores, or even individual contractors (they often have to pay to get rid of demolition waste and are more than happy to give away these materials)

Features:

- Tiny Wood Stove's Dwarf 4kw
- Solar power system: four 250-watt Renogy solar panels, connected to four 155Ah VMAX Tank deep-cycle batteries
- Nature's Head composting toilet

Stormy's custom-made couch sits across from the handicap-accessible door, offering a great view right from the living room. Hidden storage cabinets are below the cushions and in the armrests; convenient cup holders are built into the couch.

The kitchen features a large stainless steel sink and a full-size four-burner range. Hidden under the inner corner of the counter is a chest freezer that has been modified to operate as an extremely energy-efficient refrigerator. It's an easy and cheap conversion, and suits off-the-grid situations where energy use must be minimized.

The bus is heated with a small but efficient woodstove; it is easy to find branches and bits of firewood out in the wild.

Looking toward the front of the bus, notice the bathroom door, which is made from reclaimed wood. Inside the bathroom is a composting toilet and a shower made from a refurbished metal barrel that has been painted and waterproofed. These windows have been frosted for privacy, although they still let light come through.

Opposite page: The sleeping area is all the way at the back of the bus. Ladder rungs made from industrial piping lead up to the escape hatch to the roof—and the bus's roof rack and deck.

This page: The bus's steel roof rack was custom made by a metal fabrication company. The rack constituted one of the bigger costs of the bus at $4,500, but it allows the couple to haul hefty items. Rooftop solar panels are mounted on hinges at the front of the rack, and the tilt of the panels can be adjusted for maximum exposure to the sun.

DEVELOPING APPS AND HOMESCHOOLING ON A BUS

Brandon Trebitowski, a software developer and tech entrepreneur, and his wife, Ashley, are not the carefree nonconformists many might associate with bus life. Yet the Trebitowskis recently decided to move out of their 2,100-square-foot suburban home in New Mexico into a modern bus conversion they completed with the help of friends. Thanks to the wonders of the wireless Internet, their three kids are homeschooled on the road, and the family's home on wheels is also Brandon's base of operations for running a successful software company, which develops smartphone applications and employs ten people around the world.

The Trebitowskis' transition to the bus life began with Brandon's desire to get the family camping more often. They first bought a used camper trailer, which they renovated themselves. But after helping a good friend and his wife build out their bus conversion, Brandon and Ashley realized that they could do something similar as the next logical step in their quest for comfortable camping.

After searching online, the Trebitowskis purchased a 1999 Blue Bird All American school bus from a small church several states away. In total, the family spent about $24,000 for the bus and the DIY renovation, a fraction of what a new RV might cost. They drastically

---

"WE DESIGNED OUR BUS FROM THE BEGINNING TO BE AS OFF-GRID AS POSSIBLE."

---

downsized their possessions to essential things that fit onto the bus, which they nicknamed Blue Steel, and have since sold their home.

Blue Steel's design suits the family's desire to be untethered whenever needed, thanks to a 100-gallon freshwater tank and a 40-gallon gray water tank, an 800-watt solar power system and 450Ah battery bank, and two 7.5-gallon propane tanks that fuel their stove and water heater. "We designed our bus from the beginning to be as off-grid as possible," says Ashley. "Quite a bit of thought has gone into designing the water, power, waste, and propane systems to ensure that we have everything we need without being tied to a location."

The Trebitowskis now travel around in their house bus, enjoying their family adventures. Their new lifestyle gives them a lot of flexibility to move to a new locale whenever it strikes them, and their three young children benefit from seeing new places and people. In the near future, the Trebitowskis plan to purchase land in order to park and live in the bus year-round.

Opposite left: The interior of Blue Steel is bright, clean, and elegantly minimalist. Yet it also has all the hallmarks of a comfortable family home: two big couches, bunk beds for the kids, and a relatively spacious kitchen.

Opposite right: Storage has been incorporated underneath the seating to make the furniture perform more than one function. To host guests, the couches can transform into a queen-size bed.

Tips:

- Light-colored surfaces and walls help give the illusion of a bigger space
- Minimize clutter on countertops and tables by putting things away after using them
- Get a licensed electrician to double-check your electrical system setup if possible

Features:

- The 800-watt solar power system includes eight 100-watt Renogy solar panels, Morningstar's Tri-Star TS-60 charge controller, four Trojan T-105 golf cart batteries wired in series parallel, and a 3,000-watt Go Power! Pure Sine Wave Inverter
- Nature's Head composting toilet
- Atwood DV 30S three-burner propane range

The kitchen is Ashley's sanctuary, and this is a much more minimalist version of the family's previous kitchen. Because the space has been pared down, the family has changed their habits too: no more buying cute new kitchenware that sits unused, and no more letting dishes pile up before putting them in the dishwasher. Less stuff, less fuss.

There is a full-size refrigerator in its own alcove, as Ashley cooks fresh meals quite often. To gain more counter space, the sink can be covered with a fitted cutting board.

The bus's one-of-a-kind shower features a convenient ledge, white subway tiles, a raised ceiling, and a skylight, which brings in light to open up the space.

The children's bunk beds are cozy spaces for them to hang out and sleep.

At the very back is the
master bedroom, outfitted
with a very comfortable
king-size bed.

ADVENTURE OR BUST

Rising home prices, stagnating wages, growing student debt, and a brutal economic recession have made it difficult for young people to buy their own houses. So it's little wonder that millennials are actively seeking alternatives to conventional, mortgaged homes. Wanting a home of their own that wouldn't push them further into debt as they paid off their student loans, Florida-based couple Brittany and Steven Altmann looked into the possibility of building and living in a mortgage-free tiny home on wheels. "For us, it was really about the freedom the lifestyle in a smaller home could afford us," says Brittany. "The financial freedom, the freedom to live wherever we like, and the freedom to pack up and move whenever we please."

However, the couple soon realized that in order to tow a tiny home around, they would need to purchase a truck, not to mention the sizable up-front costs of building a tiny house from scratch.

So they looked into converted school buses instead. They recognized that a bus would not only be more cost-effective but it would also be much more mobile, since tiny houses on wheels can be notoriously harrowing to maneuver and tow over longer distances.

"FOR US, IT WAS REALLY ABOUT THE FREEDOM THE LIFESTYLE IN A SMALLER HOME COULD AFFORD US."

When their families caught wind of the couple's intention to convert a bus into a full-time residence, there was some opposition. "Reactions were mixed at first," recalls Brittany. "When our families first heard about our plans, they thought of the Merry Pranksters and the hippie culture of the sixties. They thought living in a tiny house meant not working hard in life. Once they calmed

down enough to listen, and learned about the benefits of living small, they came on board."

Through Craigslist, the pair found a company that maintained school buses for the local school district and purchased a 1995 International Blue Bird bus with a T444E engine and an Allison automatic transmission for $4,700.

The couple spent a year and $12,900 converting the bus themselves, meticulously documenting their expenses during the build on their blog, *Adventure or Bust*. The whole build was a challenge, since neither Brittany, a user experience (UX) designer who works remotely, nor Steven, a travel nurse, had any construction experience. Like many others, they went online to find the information they needed. "We are not builders, plumbers, or electricians," says Steven. "We learned *everything* as we went along. The tools we used were begged, borrowed, or garage sale–purchased. As a whole, it was the single most challenging thing we've ever done. Each small portion of the build alone wasn't too bad, but when you combine them all the amount of work seemed almost insurmountable."

Nevertheless, the couple persevered in completing their bus home. They moved in with their two dogs, and they now enjoy the opportunities that the reduction in monthly expenses has given them. They are able to save money, pay off their student loans more quickly, travel more often, and spend more time with each other doing the outdoor activities they love, such as hiking, biking, and fishing.

"We ultimately learned so much from the conversion, not only about building but about ourselves," says Steven. "The experience we gained during this build will follow us for the rest of our lives. It has changed our outlook on what is possible or what we are capable of."

Tips:

- Incorporate storage into furniture as much as possible to reduce clutter (for example, under the couch and bed)
- Use high-quality insulation to reduce heating and cooling costs
- Choose energy-efficient appliances
- Collect and reuse gray water for your garden
- Use the compost from the composting toilet for nonedible plants in the garden

The living room is the first zone on the bus. The L-shaped couch was custom built using plans found online and features under-seat storage. The floorplan has been kept mostly open and uncluttered to create more space, and a large flat screen television has a prominent spot on the wall opposite the couch. The layout was designed by Brittany together with Steven's cousin, Hannah, an interior designer. "With Brittany's research of tiny living spaces and Hannah's expertise on interior spaces and colors, they worked really hard to build a floorplan that utilized every inch of the bus, all while not making it feel cramped or cluttered," says Steven. "Everything has storage incorporated in it: the couch, the bed, under the sink, the 8-foot-long closet, the two 8-foot-long toolboxes outside. Even though we live full-time in the bus, our storage isn't even half full."

The kitchen features walnut counters, a full-size sink, range, refrigerator, and a combination washer-dryer. All of the appliances were chosen for their energy-efficiency. Except for the propane stove and water heater, the entire bus uses regular 120-volt appliances, rather than more expensive propane-powered RV appliances. There is a side door on the right side of the bus, which is accessible under the kitchen counter, that serves as an emergency exit. It's also useful for hauling things in and out during barbecues.

Built-in cabinets and a closet in the hallway offer a generous amount of storage.

The home has a Nature's Head composting toilet and shower stall. The compost will be ultimately used to fertilize non-edible plants in the couple's garden.

The queen-size bed at the rear of the home can be lifted with the help of hydraulic hardware, revealing storage space for outdoor gear and a 100-gallon water tank. The couple's two dogs have a sleeping space under the bed.

WHERE WE ROAM

For many, traveling the world long term seems like something to do only if you're single, financially well-off, or retired. It takes some courage to break out of those social expectations, but Scott and Emily Manning decided to do just that a few years after graduating from college. They first started with a summer-long trip across the United States and loved it so much that they wanted to continue traveling, with or without a family. So when their first baby was born, they threw conventional beliefs to the wind and set out on a 12-month journey to 12 different countries, with the little one in tow and documenting their travels online. Along the way, they learned a lot more about living with a smaller footprint.

"One central theme to the experience was how little space we needed to ourselves to do so much, both in terms of actual living space and how comfortable we felt in close quarters," recalls Scott.

The idea of "living tiny" and being able to keep one's sense of "home" no matter the location resonated strongly with the couple. Since both Scott, a digital marketing consultant, and Emily, a small business owner and photographer, were already working remotely, they wanted to build a small, portable home that could relocate with them.

"WHEN YOU'RE IN 240 SQUARE FEET, EVERYTHING HAS TO BE MULTIPURPOSE."

They shied away from the cookie-cutter feel of commercial RVs, especially after learning how they could be mechanically fickle. "We wanted something that felt inherently 'ours,' which we were not sure we could get from a typical RV. Most RVs have a different type of customer in mind when built, which is why they tend have big cushy rocking chairs in the front, a single bedroom in the back, and a lot of wasted space in the middle," says Scott.

At first, the pair looked into tiny houses, but at the suggestion of Emily's uncle, they began to consider bus conversions when they realized that the square footage would be about the same. So about a month after returning from their ambitious round-the-world trip, they found themselves a 2000 Orion V, a former transit bus, bought it for $3,000 at a public auction, and began renovations.

One major motivation behind the design was to make it feel houselike. "Less bus, more house—I was gung-ho about making the bus feel like you're stepping into an actual home, not an RV and absolutely not a city transit bus," says Emily. "There's certainly remnants of its former buslike self in the front area where the driver's seat remains, but as soon as you cross the threshold, the space really does feel that you're walking into someone's living room and kitchen."

The entire conversion process took about 10 months and cost about $35,000 (including meal costs for friends who pitched in). Like a typical RV, the Mannings' bus is designed to be plugged into the main grid and water line, and runs on 30-amp power. The couple and their young son began to live and travel in the 240-square-foot bus when renovations were almost complete. Their second child, a daughter, was born around this time.

After nearly a year of travels with the bus all over the United States, they have a third child and are now living in the bus, parked on rented land in Oregon. The couple continues to work remotely, while the whole family has made connections with other families in the area. "We wanted to find our new 'hometown,' where we could put down at least a few roots and be a part of a community," says Scott. "This is that 'hometown' we've always wanted to find."

Through their bold decision to make travel a part of their lives no matter what, Scott and Emily were able to forge a path ahead that felt right for them. But they also admit that living the bus life is not for everyone—it can be challenging, but with patience and faith, it can be done.

Tips:

- Consider installing a small tub if you have children
- Add a composting toilet to eliminate the need for a black water tank
- Find ways to make things multipurpose, or to integrate storage
- Use Murphy beds that can flip up and away during the day to free up space

Opposite page: The Mannings' main living area features a transformable open space that encompasses the living room, guest bed, kitchen, master bedroom, and playroom. Their design strategy was simple: it had to be multifunctional. "When you're in 240 square feet, everything has to be multipurpose. That's why I designed almost everything to have storage space where space was otherwise unoccupied," explains Emily.

This page: The convertible couches not only have storage hidden underneath but can also become a large guest bed. This is accomplished by pulling out wooden slats that were adapted from an existing IKEA bed.

This page: The kitchen is split into two counters on either side of the bus. It is equipped with a full-size sink, microwave, washing machine, and a folding dining table. The overhead cabinets, made by Emily's father, are handy for storing items. They also hide the bus's overhead wiring.

Opposite page: A view from the kitchen, showing the full-size refrigerator and the children's playroom, which also doubles as the master bedroom during the night.

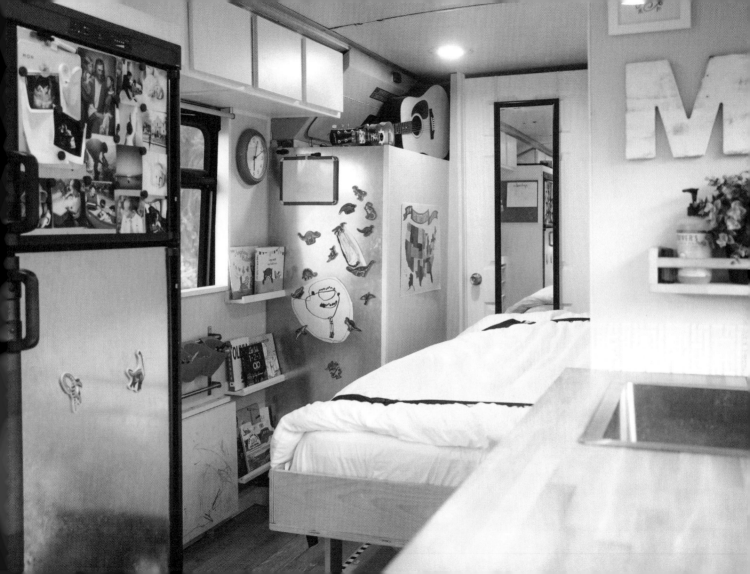

The master bed is a Murphy bed, which can be flipped up and out of the way during the day. Under the master bed are more storage benches. Both Scott and Emily have their own small closets, located to either side of the master bed.

Past the parents' bedroom is the bathroom, which has a Nature's Head composting toilet and a small, RV-style tub and shower. Since the bathroom was built over the bus's wheel wells, the toilet and shower area are elevated a few inches off the floor. "The tub was the very first item that was built into the bus—even before we put up a single wall—because we really wanted to be able to let our kids have bath time," says Emily.

At the very rear of the bus is a back room that functions as both Scott's office and the children's bedroom.

The children's bunk beds are surrounded with storage for clothes, books, and toys.

BUILDING A BUS COTTAGE AND MINIBUS RV

Sometimes when life gets tough, you get creative. During the recent economic downturn, Jeremy and Mira Thompson decided to let go of their hectic, fast-paced jobs and lifestyles in favor of something a bit simpler and more relaxed: they rented out their house and left on a year-and-a-half-long road trip in a short bus conversion they built themselves, nicknamed Minette. Jeremy leveraged his years of experience in auto body work and carpentry to complete the conversion, while Mira, a massage therapist with an eye for design, oversaw the interior layout and decor.

The couple loved living in their small but cozy bus so much that they eventually realized they wanted to convert a bigger bus so that they could start a family and live closer to their parents. It took them two years to complete the larger conversion, using a 1989 International bus with a Carpenter chassis, bought for $2,100 at an auction. The couple tackled all aspects of the project, working whenever they had time and money, and using reclaimed materials and custom building furnishings whenever possible to lower costs. They also raised the roof of the bus, significantly increasing the usable height of the interior space. Not only is the bus's rustic-modern interior elegantly conceived and constructed, its shingled, curved exterior is a whimsical delight to behold—a cottage bus parked in an idyllic setting.

"The most challenging part of the build was definitely the design and also all of the hours upon hours of custom woodwork," recalls Jeremy. "There are curves throughout, which demand a lot of attention and time. I am especially proud of the roofline that is a compound radius on the outside with a barrel ceiling on the inside. Making all those curves meet really challenged me."

Both buses are now parked on family property, situated by a lake, which the Thompsons are helping to take care of. Designed and built with future expansion in mind, the longer bus is their full-time home. They continue to use Minette as an RV, though Jeremy now has plans to convert it into a space for their two children.

But the Thompsons didn't stop at transforming two buses into comfortable living spaces. To have his own area to build things and store tools, Jeremy has also recently renovated a shipping container into a proper workshop.

Without a mortgage hanging over their heads, the family is now able to live a low-budget lifestyle in the countryside. They plan to head out on an open-ended cross-country road trip soon, and have this to say to those who might be considering something similar: "If you're just starting out, don't be too critical of your work and use the opportunity of converting a bus to learn some new skills. Don't set a deadline, because good things take time, and do it because you love doing it."

Tips:

- A removable wall panel allows you to add a future extension
- Raising the roof increases interior height; lofts can be added to provide extra square footage

The main entry is on the side, giving one the impression of entering a small home rather than a bus. One of the unique creative highlights is the sleeping alcove located at one end of the bus. It features long drawers for storing items underneath the platform, which can be rolled out in their entirety for easy access. More storage cabinets are tucked in on either side of the bed. The arched opening gives the space a magical touch, a bit of "nostalgia" that guided the couple in their overall design concept. "The nook is probably one of our favorite parts of the bus," says Jeremy. "Mira and I worked very closely on that project to meet all our needs and still be aesthetically pleasing."

Up the ladder from the sleeping alcove is one of two lofts, used for reading, playing music, or lounging around.

Opposite page: Looking toward the front of the bus, one sees the ceiling lamps that were bought from garage sales and restored with new wiring. The flooring is reclaimed Douglas fir, bought from a local demolition company and coated with a low-VOC (volatile organic compounds), water-based polyurethane that doesn't off-gas toxins. The bus's signature round window was hand-crafted by Jeremy, and is actually part of a removable panel that will allow the couple to connect the bus to a future extension, such as a sunroom or shipping container.

This page: The bus's antique woodstove gives the space a rustic charm. The loveseat across from the hearth hides a bit of storage space under its seat.

The kitchen is equipped with a full-size range, a deep farmhouse sink, a restored vintage refrigerator, and two counters, part of which forms a breakfast nook.

The bathroom is located near the front of the bus, and is split into two parts on either side of the home—one with the flush toilet, and the other for the full-size shower. If the family decides to live off the grid someday, the toilet area can be converted to hold a composting toilet instead. The bus uses an on-demand water heater.

Inside the Thompsons' minibus RV, which was the couple's first project and is now used as the family RV. Purchased at an auction for $2,500, Minette features a multifunctional design. There's a bed, kitchen, woodstove, three-way refrigerator that runs on propane, 12-volt or 120-volt current, and DIY composting toilet.

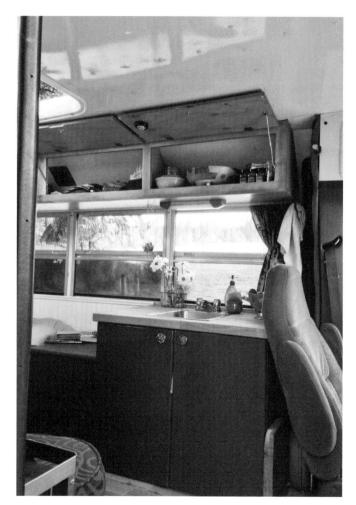

Jeremy's latest project is retrofitting a recycled shipping container into a cottage-style workshop. The structure sports the same whimsical, shingled aesthetic as the main house bus. It features an insulating green roof done with sod and a functional workshop interior.

BIG BERTHA

Can a bus be a home that takes you out of the "rent trap"?

With housing and living costs rising in major metropolitan areas, many young families are looking for alternatives—whether it's living in smaller homes, co-ownership, or yes, even self-built homes on wheels.

Hoping to get out of the precarious situation of living paycheck to paycheck, Brian and Starla Sullivan began looking for alternatives to the expensive yet drab two-bedroom Seattle apartment they were renting. They were new parents and Brian had recently found a job in aerospace manufacturing a few towns away, and so the couple wanted to move somewhere quieter and closer to Brian's job.

They considered purchasing a conventional RV at first. But they soon discarded that idea after realizing that RVs are generally not very durable and aren't designed for full-time living. Tiny houses on trailers were appealing, but they seemed too difficult to maneuver. Dis-

couraged, the Sullivans continued to hunt for apartments for several months without much success. But then they chanced upon an online video about a bus conversion. It was an "aha" moment for the pair. Living in such a way would allow them to reduce their expenses, to design and build a home of their own that suited their needs as a growing family, and to have

---

"WE WANTED TO TAKE CONTROL OF OUR LIVES."

---

a house on wheels that could be easily moved. It seemed like a crazy idea—yet, somehow, it seemed right. "We wanted to take control of our lives," says Brian. "We wanted to *make* another option where there didn't seem to be any other options."

The couple began to shop around for retired school buses through government auctions, online classifieds, and marketplaces. Finally they found the

perfect bus, a 1996 Blue Bird for $2,800, at a local dealership. They were then able to find a rural RV storage lot where they could store and work on the bus during the weekends for the next year, eventually registering it as an RV.

Though neither had building experience, they used online resources and their local library to help them along in the process. Starla, who studied interior design, is the mastermind behind the bus's multifunctional and efficient layout, which has been designed to maximize the small amount of space available. To increase the utility of the interior space, all the furniture and appliances are multifunctional. Reclaimed materials were used whenever possible, and materials and finishes were chosen for their washability and eco-friendliness—important features for a family with young children. For instance, the family installed carpet tiles, which can be individually replaced if one becomes soiled. To accommodate the routines and habits of their growing family, they conceived an adapt-

able interior that will eventually "grow" along with them. To keep interior temperatures comfortable year-round and to prevent water condensation from forming on the metal surfaces during the winter, the bus has also been fully insulated with spray foam. Dimmable and energy-efficient LED lighting has been incorporated throughout, and the bus uses solar power for its appliances and gadgets. All told, the Sullivans spent around $25,000 for tools, materials, appliances, and a new paint job for their bus home, which they have lovingly nicknamed Big Bertha.

Since moving into their bus conversion, the Sullivans have welcomed two more children into the world. This family of five is now living full-time in their new home, on an idyllic piece of rented land beside a nature preserve, just 20 minutes outside of Seattle. As opposed to a punishing, hours-long daily commute, Brian now only needs 15 minutes to drive to work in the family car.

Living this way has allowed the Sullivans to pay off debts, save money, and spend more time together as a family. Their plan now is to save enough money to realize bigger dreams in the future. "Down the road, we would love to buy our own land and dabble with experimental architecture," says Brian. "Cob houses, earth-bag structures, and Earthships. We want our children to help in this process hands-on and gain another valuable life skill. Perhaps they would even want to build their own tiny homes on our land and we can then be close to our grandchildren too."

Tips:

- Use reclaimed materials to reduce costs
- Choose nontoxic, durable materials and easy-to-clean finishes
- Design your home to adapt and expand along with your family

Features:

- Dickinson P-9000 propane furnace
- Bosch Speed Oven: multifunctional built-in wall oven that can microwave, toast, and bake
- Duxtop portable induction cooktop
- Altered Nozzle: water-saving faucet that mists or sprays water, reducing water use by 85 to 98 percent
- Eva-dry E-333 Renewable Mini Dehumidifier: a rechargeable unit that absorbs moisture to prevent mold, designed for small spaces

Two multipurpose upholstered seating benches are on either side of the main living area, and each has storage space hidden under the seats. The benches also incorporate slats that can slide out to form a full-size bed for guests. There is a wall-mounted television screen for family movie nights. This is also where the family dines, thanks to a foldaway table made out of reclaimed bamboo. The table can be configured in various ways, and it can be stored out of sight when it's not needed.

The Sullivans love preparing healthy home-cooked meals, and their kitchen features two large counters. These flat surfaces are also great for folding laundry and doing activities with the kids.

A wire shelf above one of the counters can be used for both storing and drying dishes. To eliminate clutter, dried goods are stored away in large drawers under the counters. The Sullivans deliberately chose energy-efficient appliances, such as their multipurpose microwave, which also functions as a toaster and convection oven. Energy-efficient portable induction stovetops can be stowed away to save more space.

The kitchen also includes the bus's source of heating—a compact and ultra-efficient Dickinson Marine propane furnace.

The Sullivans' bathroom includes a composting toilet. This is a kind of waterless toilet, which when maintained correctly, eliminates odors and transforms waste into a nutrient-rich fertilizer that can be used on nonedible plants. The shower uses a deep horse trough as a basin, perfect for giving baths to the children. The family uses a high-efficiency washing machine, and to minimize electricity use, clothes and cloth diapers are air-dried on a foldaway drying rack.

Next on the bus comes the children's sleeping bunks and play area. The clever adaptable design modifies the children's beds into "play bunks" that have windows, ladders, and a safety gate, to give the impression of a playhouse. One of the beds can be quickly transformed into a large play surface merely by removing the mattress. All bunks are built for full-length single beds, so they will fit the boys as they grow. Toys and clothes are neatly stored under the beds.

At the rear of the bus is Starla and Brian's bedroom. The bed here is elevated on a platform, built over the bus's rear engine. The overarching theme of multifunctionality and hidden storage is seen here as well, through the use of under-bed storage drawers and fold-down tables that can quickly transform the bedroom into another workspace.

The very front of the bus is separated from the rest of the home by a wall and door. This particular design feature isn't seen on many bus conversions, but it helps to create a more comfortable and thermally insulated interior. "Having a partition wall to close off the front area, where the front door and windshield are located, has really helped regulate the temperature in the bus and creates a separate space that feels more like a home and less like a vehicle," says Starla.

This area contains the driver's seat, home office, and an occasional play area. It's also where the family stores their coats and shoes.

LIVING BUS LIFE
TO THE FULLEST

Our lives—and our perception of our lives—can change completely in a catastrophic moment. It may be the loss of a loved one, a sudden accident, or it could be literally an earthquake, as it was in the case of Andrew Cleverley and Amber Mackintosh, a couple from New Zealand.

The earthquake that changed everything was the 6.3 magnitude event that struck the city of Christchurch in February 2011. Andrew and Amber were 25 floors up in a building that was only a few miles from the epicenter. The quake caused severe damage to many structures, including the building they were in. For several terrifying hours, the couple attempted to find their way out as it leaned dangerously to one side. The fire escape was destroyed. Neither knew whether they were going to survive before they were eventually rescued off a neighboring roof.

Needless to say, they were traumatized by the ordeal. A few years after surviving the earthquake, the couple welcomed the arrival of a son and daughter. But because they were residing in Auckland, one of the most expensive cities in the world, their cost of living was quite high. That meant working long, stressful hours every week in their full-time jobs, while the children remained in day care, leaving them very little time to spend together.

Finally, the couple reached a breaking point in the daily juggling act. They realized they were not "free" in the full sense of the word, and wanted to find a way to spend more time together as a family, while having great experiences and living life to the fullest—because it literally could end at any moment.

Andrew and Amber began to research ways to reduce their expenses and find an easy way to travel. Converting a bus into a motorhome seemed like the best way to go. The couple found a 36-foot 1987 Volvo B6FA 6-liter turbo diesel bus—previously a city transit and school bus—and purchased it for $7,000.

They then embarked on a year of renovations, working almost every weekend and every night after work on the project. Andrew, who did the bulk of the conversion, did not have previous experience in construction. He learned how to build and how to install plumbing and electrical systems through YouTube videos and other online resources. For safety, they hired a professional to install the propane system. For the interior renovations, the couple spent about $15,000.

Since completing the bus conversion, they have gradually phased themselves out of their jobs and are now traveling full-time around New Zealand. By getting out of the "rent trap," they were able to reduce their expenses to $400 a month. To create new revenue streams, they are exploring several location-independent small business options, but their income doesn't have to be very high to cover their new cost of living. "The beauty of reducing your expenses so much is that you can reduce your income a lot," says Andrew.

For the moment, the family is taking the time to enjoy a slower, less stressful version of life, while keeping their future options open as much as possible by saving money, possibly to buy land to start a small homestead. For now, Andrew says, "the kids love their new home and really enjoy getting into the outdoors."

For those considering the same path, Andrew has this bit of sage advice: "Don't be afraid of starting the project. You'll learn as you go and mistakes can be fixed and imperfections can either be covered or become part of the character of the bus. The biggest thing is to just make sure it's safe." He adds, "Do heaps of research and don't just take just one person's advice or opinion as gospel, because there are so many ways of doing things. It's just a big puzzle and the problems get easier to solve the further into the build you get, because your skill and confidence grows."

Tips:

- To check for leaks on a potential bus purchase, take it through a truck wash and see if any water appears inside
- Safety first: Get a professional to double-check or install things like propane lines and electrical systems
- Gather research from many different sources
- Reduce expenses first so you need less income
- Minimizing belongings means more living space
- Use a laundromat instead of installing a washer and dryer; you save space, water, energy, and waste-water storage

Features:

- Little Cracker woodstove
- 850-watt solar power system, with 960Ah Century Yuasa storage battery
- 66-gallon freshwater tank, 21-gallon toilet-flushing tank (can use nonpotable gray water to flush)
- Nature's Head composting toilet
- Rainwater can be harvested from roof
- Bus engine can run on recycled waste vegetable oil (WVO)
- Samsung Digital Inverter Compressor fridge

Opposite page: The main living spaces include a sitting area, a dining and work area, a kitchen, a bathroom, and bedrooms. The layout is mostly open in the front, encompassing the shared spaces where the family congregates.

This page: To save space, the couch has storage hidden underneath, and can be turned into a bed for a guest to sleep over. The couch also has seat belts installed under the cushions.

An efficient Little Cracker woodstove heats the entire space and serves as an extra cooking surface. Firewood is stored in a small cabinet right beside the woodstove. The dining area has a foldable table, which also doubles as a workspace. Under the table there is more storage for the children's toys.

The kitchen includes a huge counter, a gas-powered stove, oven, and water heater, as well as a full-size energy-efficient refrigerator that runs on solar power. The pantry features big metal racks that can slide out for easy access and visibility.

The children's bunk beds are on one side of the hallway. Both of the bunks have windows for a nice view out. On the other side of the hallway is the bathroom, split into two areas, one containing the composting toilet, the other containing the sink, shower, and storage.

The master bedroom at the back has a full-size bed. The exits here are still operational.

THE PROFESSOR AND HER CHAMPION

One can infer a lot about a culture and society from the way their members interact with their natural environment. Each culture represents a distillation of generations of inherited knowledge and particular beliefs that arise from the relationship they have with nature.

This concurrent evolution between nature and human cultures, of "biocultural diversity," is the area of study ethnoecologist Jeanine Pfeiffer has been researching for the last 30-odd years. Jeanine has traveled and worked in more than 30 different countries, but she has been teaching for the last 15 years at San José State University in California.

So it may be surprising to discover that Jeanine lives in a converted shuttle bus called The Champion. Like many, Jeanine was struggling with rising living costs and miserably high rents in Northern California, and was looking for alternatives to the expensive bedroom she was renting in a shared house. "After a series of traumatic experiences with unscrupulous landlords, resulting in even more traumatic and costly moves, I began researching tiny homes," recounts Jeanine. "I looked into buying a boat or a steel shipping container and converting it, but I was hampered by a lack of funds, and the learning curve for managing either of those options seemed too steep."

Then one day Jeanine spotted a gleaming white shuttle bus turning the corner, and it occurred to her that it looked rather handsome, was probably well-equipped with its own heating and air conditioning, and was likely much more maneuverable than a huge school bus.

The same day, Jeanine cashed out part of her pension and began the hunt online for a suitable shuttle bus. Within a month, she'd found a 2007 Ford Champion Challenger with relatively low mileage for $15,000. She then hired a father-son team to help her take out the old seats and install new flooring for $500. A good friend, Virginia Thigpen, provided Jeanine with crucial design ideas and financial help during the build.

The day after the flooring was done, Jeanine held a huge yard sale to sell her nonessential belongings. A few days later she brought her furnishings and other possessions onboard the now refurbished Champion and bid farewell to her landlord. Because Jeanine didn't need to build anything new, and had secured her existing furniture to the floor, the entire conversion and move-in process took only a week. All of the decor and trinkets now on the bus have some kind of sentimental and cultural significance: a traditional woven blanket from artisans hailing locally or from afar, or a plant from the family she stays with when she travels to Indonesia. "Each carefully curated piece has a story, a memory, a meaning," says Jeanine.

For Jeanine, a shuttle bus conversion made more sense than building a more

Previous page: Jeanine's layout in her bus home continues to evolve over time. This photograph shows an earlier configuration that was simple but well-suited for her needs. It includes large windows that let light pour in; a home office area; plenty of carefully chosen plants to liven up the space and purify the air; a modified lofted IKEA bed to increase usable space and storage; a wardrobe; a space for her harp; her dog, Lusa; and a custom-designed odorless dry toilet and shower space, hidden behind a shower curtain.

This page: The Champion shuttle bus prior to and during the simple renovation.

expensive tiny home, or retrofitting a mass-manufactured RV, or converting a school bus, even though others didn't seem to understand at first. "Initially, I was repulsed by suggestions of 'Why don't you convert a school bus?' because most of the conversions I saw were unattractive or poorly executed," says Jeanine. "Logistically, I couldn't afford a new paint job on a school bus, which would otherwise stand out like a sore thumb, and the average school bus was hard to park because of its length.

"This is why it was such an epiphany when I realized that I could purchase a shiny, white, streamlined shuttle bus. This bus didn't need a new paint job. It was short enough to fit into two standard-size parking spaces and could also fit into the maximum 25-foot-long state park campground spaces. It is relatively easy to drive, especially with the already-installed back-up camera. Its exterior looked new and clean enough to not be discriminated against in RV parks that frown upon school bus conversions or older motorhomes."

There's also the aspect of living more lightly, even if it's in a vehicle. Jeanine goes on to say: "In keeping with my principles as an environmental scientist who teaches about climate change, I live as low-impact as possible: I use very little water, I create less than two trash bags

---

"I LIVE AS LOW-IMPACT AS POSSIBLE."

---

of waste each year, I am frugal with my electricity use, and I bike and use public transportation as often as possible."

In addition, Jeanine uses a mix of low-wattage appliances to cook and to heat and cool her home, depending on whether she's off-grid or plugged into the main grid. She deliberately chose not to include propane appliances in her setup. She uses a small electric heater during cooler months and an energy-efficient, portable air conditioner. When Jeanine is off the grid, she uses one 45-watt solar panel, a 300-watt inverter, and a house battery.

Besides these changes to daily habits, Jeanine is now aiming to "balance out" personal carbon emissions that cannot be avoided—such as those produced when driving The Champion around to relocate every few weeks to different RV parks or properties of friends throughout the region. "This year I am going a step further and becoming carbon-neutral by completely offsetting my carbon footprint by funding the planting of culturally significant trees in the homelands of my adopted tribe in Indonesia, the Tado," she explains.

While some may point out the contradictions of aspiring toward a carbon-neutral lifestyle while living in a fuel-guzzling bus, the reality is that everything we do, purchase, or eat has some kind of carbon footprint. The

Members of the Tado community and their reforestation efforts in Indonesia.

goal is to become aware of this and to start where we are, taking small steps toward living more sustainably whenever possible.

For example, though Jeanine does call a bus her home, she only drives it about 1,000 miles per year. Jeanine was one of the first professors in her department to pioneer teaching her courses online, meaning that she doesn't have to commute, and neither do her students. Over time, Jeanine has consciously modified her daily habits in many small but meaningful ways to reduce her overall environmental footprint. "Being carbon-neutral means that I carefully account for all aspects of my lifestyle, calculate the carbon dioxide tonnage that I'm contributing to the atmosphere, and convert that tonnage into fast-growing plants, such as bamboo or grasses, that are planted by the Tado community," explains Jeanine. "In other words, I must somehow generate living, photosynthesizing plants that remove carbon dioxide from the atmosphere and convert it into oxygen at a rate higher than my personal contributions. If we all did this, as individuals, businesses, organizations, and corporations, we would bring climate change to a halt—eventually."

Besides downsizing her carbon footprint, for Jeanine living the bus life is about being able to live more fully, without the burden of financial worries. Since moving into The Champion, she has reduced her expenses to only a few hundred dollars a month. In 2017, the mobility of Jeanine's home also allowed her to quickly evacuate and return later when wildfires swept across Northern California.

"Instead of calling myself semi-retired, I say that I'm on semi-permanent vacation," says Jeanine. "As long as I am careful with my finances, this is a much less stressful way to live than being a wage slave where 30 to 40 percent of my income goes to support the high rents and mortgages typical of Northern California. Because I have vastly reduced my monthly fixed expenses, I am able to maintain a lifestyle where I work about 20 hours a week, with my remaining time free to spend on more creative pursuits."

Tips:

- Outsource the plumbing: consider installing a waterless toilet, or use the restroom and shower facilities available in state and national parks, fairgrounds, and Kampgrounds of America (KOA)
- Have contingency plans for what appliances to use when you are plugged into the main grid, when you are using solar power, or when you use nothing at all (examples: have a camping stove as a backup to an induction stovetop; have a cooler as a backup to your refrigerator)
- Propane is flammable, so it requires extra care; consider skipping the use of propane-powered appliances in favor of other options
- You can offset the inevitable carbon emissions of living in a vehicle by reducing your environmental footprint elsewhere: by biking or using public transportation; using solar power; reducing water use and waste; reusing materials; and supporting environmental projects

"PRIORITY SEATING FOR PERSONS WITH
DISABILITIES. OTHER PASSENGERS
SHOULD MAKE THESE SEATS AVAILABLE
TO THOSE WHO WISH TO USE THEM"

Having a home office with organized storage was key. "Because I am a scientist-scholar with a ton of files and side projects, I had to incorporate significant desk and office storage space," says Jeanine. "This is achieved by installing filing boxes and wooden storage boxes beneath my glass desk and my modified loft bed."

Jeanine's favorite red chair and the dresser that she uses as a kitchen counter and pantry.

Left: The Champion among the redwoods in Hendy Woods State Park.

Right: Plants are an integral part of Jeanine's design for her home, giving it the impression of an eclectic and vibrant apartment on wheels. "I specifically designed the space to support palm trees (in self-watering IKEA pots) at each end of the bus, hanging plants in the front of the bus, outside hanging planters on the back door of the bus, and a box of succulents in the side front window."

THE MIDWEST WANDERERS

Wanting to travel and see more of the country beyond their quiet suburban hometown near Chicago, Illinois, Luke and Rachel Davis decided to take a huge leap of faith. They converted an old school bus into an impressive home, quit their jobs, sold their 1,500-square-foot house, and took to the road. They have been traveling ever since with their young daughter and dog.

The couple happened to learn about bus conversions and the alluring possibilities of the "bus life" through an acquaintance. At first, it seemed like a far-fetched idea, but they were intrigued by the possibility of being able to travel while bringing their home along with them. After some consideration of whether they could make it work, the Davises found a retired school bus online for $4,000.

The 37-foot-long bus, which they fondly call Walter, is a 1992 AmTran Genesis bus, equipped with a diesel engine, automatic transmission, and air brakes. Once you step beyond its buslike shell, Wal-ter's interior feels roomy and well-lit, like a real home. The Davises made a number of big changes to the bus to make it more spacious and self-sufficient. These modifications included raising the roof and installing a 900-watt solar panel system, a composting toilet, and a 100-gallon freshwater tank.

"WORKING AS A TEAM IS ONE OF THE MOST IMPORTANT ASPECTS OF LIVING TOGETHER IN A SMALL SPACE."

Luke did much of the renovation himself, which was made easier thanks to his years of experience working in the construction industry. To save money, the family bought reclaimed items, including double-paned RV windows, an awning, a water pump, and almost-new but heavily discounted appliances from an RV sal-vage yard. They used recycled bamboo flooring and barn wood for their accent wall and kitchen counters. In total, the couple estimate that they spent about $30,000 for their renovations.

So far they have been enjoying their new rhythm immensely. Instead of working long days, or spending hours maintaining their former home in the suburbs, they now get to spend an abundance of time together as a family, traveling and embracing new experiences. But it's not without challenges. "Bus life can quickly fall apart when we aren't all working as a team," notes Luke. "We've learned that this is one of the most important aspects of living together in a small space. Also, being off-grid, we don't often feel like paying to stay at a campground when we already have everything we need—power, water, and so on—so finding places to boondock or park can be tricky at times, but we almost always find a way."

Thanks to the huge reduction in monthly

expenses brought on by moving into the bus conversion, the Davises are debt-free and are currently funding their travels using money saved from selling their house. Their ultimate plan is to find another place to set down roots again—someday. For now, they continue to wander and experience the wider world around them, for the sheer love of it.

Tips:

- Buy items and appliances at cheaper prices from RV salvage yards (sometimes these are almost new but marked down significantly)
- Raising the roof increases usable space and design possibilities, such as creating stacked spaces

The couple raised the roof almost 2 feet on their renovated 240-square-foot home, adding a significant amount of headroom to the interior space. This also permitted them to add a lofted sleeping mezzanine at the back of the bus.

A well-appointed kitchen was essential for Rachel, a baker who was running her own business. The house bus kitchen therefore has full-size appliances, including a propane range and a multi-modal refrigerator that runs on both propane and regular household current. The counters are made from salvaged barn beams, the cabinetry features handmade and embossed leather pulls, and the dining table is made out of locally reclaimed walnut.

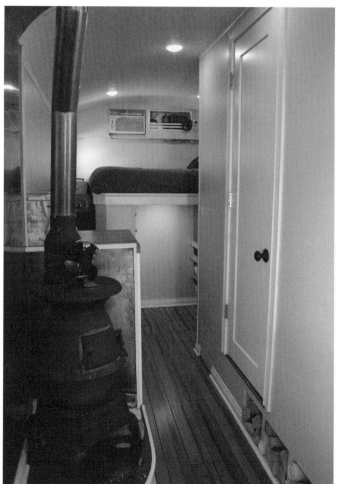

The family living room centers around a large, comfortable three-seater couch that can convert into an extra bed. Right across is a refurbished cast-iron potbellied stove, which is fed with firewood stored in the built-in cubbies directly under the bathroom.

The bathroom has a composting toilet and a metal-lined alcove for the shower-tub. "We are able to stretch our 100-gallon freshwater tank to last two weeks by utilizing an extremely low-flow shower head and, of course, treating every drop like it matters," says Luke.

The raised ceiling means that the family's sleeping area can be stacked in a space-efficient configuration, with the daughter's sleeping nook and storage drawers on the bottom and the parents' bed lofted up on top, and accessible by stair (next page).

The solar power system took some figuring out. "Surprisingly, the information for designing and building an off-grid solar power system—even in 2017—isn't all that abundant and seems to vary quite a bit," says Luke. "With enough homework, we were able to pull it off. Also, building anything inside of an old school bus offers plenty of resistance, but it can be done."

THE YETIBUS

Not surprisingly, the freedom offered by living the bus life appeals to individuals as well as couples and families. Kyle Volkman is one of these adventurous souls who has chosen to live in converted vehicles for the last decade. After his high school graduation in Idaho, Kyle spent two summers traveling in a van conversion and renting apartments during the winter months. But as an avid outdoor enthusiast who wanted to be outside as much as possible, Kyle soon wanted to live this flexible lifestyle year-round. So he began to look into the larger space offered by bus conversions, with the aim of converting one into a more eco-friendly vehicle that would run on vegetable oil. As a fuel, waste vegetable oil (WVO) produces less carbon monoxide and particulate matter than diesel, and is a recycled waste product that can be abundantly sourced from restaurants, fast food outlets, and factories.

Kyle's home, the Yetibus, is a 1986 30-foot-long Blue Bird bus. The fully insulated interior features a raised roof and a simple but functional design: Kyle's skill as a trained carpenter shines through in the well-crafted woodwork and cabinetry.

But what is hidden is just as important as what is seen. After a recent remodel of the Yetibus, Kyle got a large custom-made veggie fuel tank mounted

---

"THE BIGGEST PERK FOR ME IS THE FREEDOM."

---

under the bus and rewired the whole system. The bus is now equipped with an International DT466 diesel engine that can run on discarded veggie oil. "Burning a nontaxed, renewable fuel makes me proud because I'm acting on my convictions," explains Kyle. "I'm able to travel for much less money, contribute minimally to climate change, and not support the fossil fuel industry."

Kyle's plan is to install a 500-watt solar power system with two Marathon AGM batteries, but for now the bus can be plugged in. "All my outlets in the bus are wired through a circuit breaker box and an external plug-in, so I can run my extension cord and plug into 'shore power' [the main electrical grid] while parked," says Kyle. Once Kyle has his solar photovoltaic panels installed, he will be able to join these two sources of power, using a power inverter to convert the 12-volt direct current from the photovoltaic system into the regular 120 volts of alternating current.

Kyle's goal is to someday purchase land for the Yetibus. But for now, his bus allows him to play, travel, and work more freely: besides traveling around to do custom carpentry jobs and vehicle conversions for others, Kyle works as a photographer and musician. "The biggest perk for me is the freedom," says Kyle. "I've tried to structure a life where I can work on a project-to-project basis

that's centered around what I love to do: traveling and enjoying the outdoors—snowboarding, climbing, mountain biking, surfing, and hiking. Also important is acting on my beliefs—through the vegetable oil to diesel conversion, solar power, recycling, conserving energy—and knowing that I'm doing all that I can to lower my carbon footprint and protect the planet I love is very satisfying."

Left: The layout of the bus is open, and partitioning walls have been kept to a minimum to give a sense of spaciousness. Energy-efficient LED lighting is used throughout to minimize energy use.

Tips:

- Minimize partitions to keep the floor plan open and maximize space
- Consider installing appliances or equipment made for marine applications
- Try to buy your bus directly from a school district or police auction; the more hands a bus passes through, the higher the chance of mechanical problems and the higher the prices

Features:

- Isotemp water heater (works as an engine-coolant and hot-water heat exchanger)
- Norcold three-way refrigerator (runs on propane, 12-volt, and 120-volt)
- Air Head composting toilet (no black water produced, odorless)
- Maxxfan 12-volt ventilation fan to improve interior air circulation
- Wood heating, with an efficient woodstove designed for use in small spaces (to be upgraded to the Tiny Wood Stove)

The couch has hidden storage underneath the seat, as well as behind in the backrest. It can also transform into a guest bed by unfolding some support fins from underneath, flipping out a hinged wooden platform, and rearranging the cushions on top to form a bed.

The well-lit kitchen has a propane cooktop and oven. The open shelves keep frequently used pantry items within easy access, while spring-loaded barrel bolts secure the cabinet doors above for minimal vibration while driving. Water from the sink faucet can run using either a 12-volt water pump or, to conserve electricity, a foot pump. Beneath the sink is the Isotemp water heater that's typically used on sailboats, which simultaneously functions as an engine-coolant and hot-water heat exchanger. "As I drive, hot engine coolant is looped through a heat exchanger in the 7-gallon tank, making for a tank full of scalding hot water, which turns into a lot more hot water once it's diluted down to a usable temperature," says Kyle. "The water heater helps to cool the engine too, which is always a plus."

This page: The dinette is where Kyle eats meals and works on his laptop. There is storage for Kyle's tools underneath the bench seats. The tabletop features a hand-drawn map of the Pacific Northwest that's been glued on top and then coated with epoxy.

Opposite page: The bus uses a compact and ultra-efficient woodstove that's specially designed to fit into and heat up small spaces.

At the very back of the bus is an alcove where the bedroom is located. The focal point is the mural on the back wall, painted in wood stain by a friend of Kyle's. Thev bedroom holds a large mattress, wall shelving, and a small closet to hang clothes along the partition facing the mural.

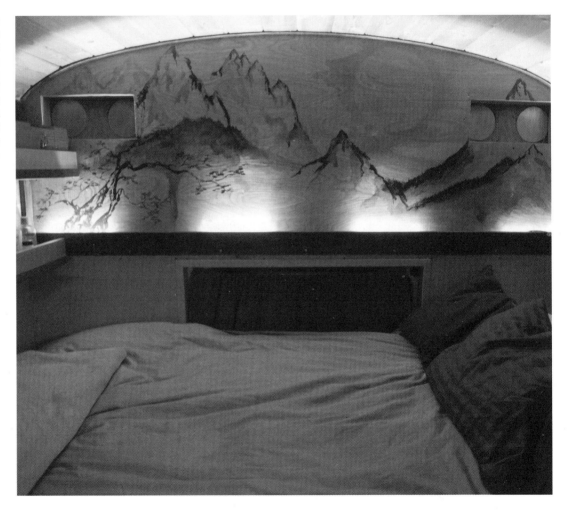

At the front of the bus, the driver's seat is crowned with a sunlike mural painted by Kyle himself. There is more built-in shelving here to store books, as well as a custom-made sound system with speakers and a large subwoofer for booming out music while on the road.

BY THE GRACE
OF THE QUEEN
OF PEACE

It's one thing to build a house bus for yourself, and quite another to build buses for others as your full-time occupation, as Denver, Colorado–based professional bus homebuilder Charles Kern has been doing for the last few years.

Charles himself lives in a converted 1982 Blue Bird bus with an International Harvester chassis, which he revamped over a period of nine months at an overall cost of $27,000. Charles's bus was formerly used to transport kids in a local school district and then to ferry around a church youth group for Denver's Queen of Peace Catholic Parish—hence, the bus's regal moniker, The Queen of Peace.

The Queen's interior is cozy and warm, thanks to the natural textures of its wooden surfaces, some of the wood sustainably sourced from trees felled by crews battling the pine beetle infestation in Colorado's forests. Instead of leaving this "beetle kill" wood as potential kindling to fuel devastating wildfires in the region, this distinctly patterned wood is harvested to use as building material and to create beautiful furniture. Other items in The Queen, such as the cabinets, were made from wood salvaged from demolition sites around Denver. In addition to the bus's simple but functional layout, it is equipped with a robust solar power system, water tanks, and a composting toilet, permitting it to go off-grid indefinitely.

Charles's motivation to transform a bus into an energy-efficient home was simple: as a broke 20-year-old philosophy student who needed a place to live and who knew a thing or two about fixing up buses, it seemed like a good idea. But even before he finished renovating his own house bus, others were approaching him to convert buses for them.

So far, Charles and his company, Art Builders Guild, have transformed six vehicles into homes of varying sizes and styles for clients. They all feature excellent craftsmanship, marvelous details, and clever design strategies to save space, while offering a glimpse into the immense creativity and skill Charles and his team employ to make their clients' dreams come true. Making the decision to convert his own bus has led Charles to bring that same joyful vision of life to others—by building bus homes, teaching workshops, and even hosting a television special on bus conversions. If there ever was an apostle for the bus life, it would be Charles.

"Living on the bus has taught me a lot," says Charles. "Most importantly, it taught me how to convert a school bus into a fully livable home on wheels, which I now do for a living. The irony is, now that I live on wheels, I have a shop where I build them for others so I don't have the nomadic lifestyle I once imagined when I built The Queen. Things have been busy and when I have the opportunity to catch my breath between it all, I am grateful for all the ways the bus provides for me."

Tips:

- Incorporate a Murphy bed on hinges that can fold up and out of the way, to free up space during the day
- Convert a chest freezer into a super-efficient refrigerator and put it under the counter on rails
- Instead of latches, bolts, or cords, use extra-strong magnets to secure things
- Extra storage space can be hidden under the floor, using trapdoors

The Queen's main living area includes a woodstove that can heat the whole space, a futon sofa bed, and a custom-built sound system built in right above the driver's seat.

CAPACITY 65 PASSENGERS

BLUE BIRD BODY CO.

Charles's kitchen has a propane range and refrigerator on one side. On the other side is a sink and wall-mounted dish-drying rack, which serves for drying and storing dishes. The cabinetry uses skillful joinery done by Charles's friend.

The bedroom is at the very rear of the bus. The bed is a Murphy-style piece, which can flip up into the wall and out of the way, freeing up the entire floor.

This page: The Queen is equipped with a 1,875-watt solar panel array—more than enough power for a vehicle of this size, and sufficient to run lights, gadgets, the water heater, and the air-conditioning during the summer.

Opposite page: The Queen is currently parked on a friend's farm property just outside the city.

This is Lucy, a 1995 AmTran Genesis school bus conversion done by Art Builders Guild and commissioned by a hat maker. It's her off-grid studio, home, and mobile store. Interesting features include custom oak and walnut cabinetry with a recycled copper backsplash and a chest freezer that has been converted into an extremely efficient refrigerator that uses only one-tenth of the electricity of a regular refrigerator. It is placed on a custom steel rack that can roll in and out of the kitchen counter.

This is a bus conversion built by Art Builders Guild for a family of three. The kitchen occupies the central space and features a live-edge counter, with the raw, unmilled edge of the lumber exposed. A sleeping loft is all the way in the back for the family's four-year-old child, and it is accessible via a set of stairs that double as storage drawers.

Dubbed The Success Express, this conversion was done for a performing artist who crafts and sells fire-spinning props all over the country. This bus is packed with clever space-saving furniture and ideas. It has a custom slide-out sofa bed, a table that folds out of a box on the wall, a combination washer-dryer, and expansive storage space under the bus. There's also an elevated platform for the bed at the rear of the bus, while cleverly hidden trapdoors in the bedroom floor create even more underfloor storage.

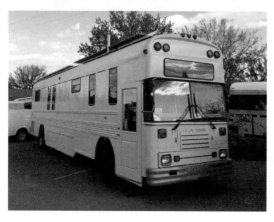

The Dirt Turtle bus was built for a nomadic couple in collaboration with shipbuilders in Maine. The results are truly exceptional: it has a nautical-inspired design, using heart pine carpentry, and lots of technologically advanced features, such as radiant-floor heating, solar panels, and other gadgetry, all requiring more than a mile of wiring cables. There's no other bus like it out there.

CHOOSING AND RENOVATING A HOUSE BUS

Before even considering a bus conversion project, it's important to ask yourself why you want to do it. Is it the allure of being more mobile, of being able to travel almost anywhere at a moment's notice? Is it the practicality of having more financial freedom, of being able to live mortgage free? Or might it be the satisfaction that comes from successfully tackling a challenging, do-it-yourself project?

If you've done your research and decide bus conversion is the way to go, consider the following pages to be a basic guide on the major steps of converting a bus into a comfortable living space on wheels.

Note: This book is not an exhaustive guide to all the technical aspects of bus conversions—only the basics are laid out here. For more details, consult the resources on page 231, visit online forums, and familiarize yourself with online video tutorials for do-it-yourself construction tips. The Internet is a treasure trove of information, and you'll discover that there are various methods for finishing any given task. There is no one path to completing a bus conversion—it depends on your needs, your budget, local regulations, available materials, and so on.

GETTING STARTED

Choosing Your Bus

Before getting started, you need a bus. First determine what kind of bus best suits your needs. Are you planning to travel over long distances often? Will the bus be occupied with a single person or two, or do you have a family with children? How do you plan to use it (as a part-time travel rig or as a full-time, mostly stationary home)? Where do you plan to travel (do you have to consider winterizing your bus for cold weather)?

Buses come in a wide variety of makes, models, and sizes. They range from around 20 to 25 feet for the shorter school or shuttle buses to 45 feet for interstate motorcoaches and transit buses. Most buses come in at around 8 feet wide. There are wider models available on the market (more than 100 inches), but these can be difficult to drive and are more costly to purchase and maintain. Shorter buses are easier to maneuver and park, and they are more suitable for shorter family trips or for two people long term. By contrast, longer buses are more challenging to drive and park, but they are more spacious and are better-suited for larger families. The size of the vehicle is also related to gross vehicle weight rating (GVWR), both factors that will determine what type of license you need to drive it (see page 226).

Here are the most common types of buses available:

- **School Buses:**

  These are the most widely available type of bus, and with a bit of careful shopping, you can find one in fair condition for a few thousand dollars or less. School buses are characterized by lower ceilings and typically do not have built-in storage bays underneath. One of the biggest advantages of school buses is that the big manufacturers use a common truck chassis, meaning that parts will be easy to find. School buses also have a higher ground clearance than other types of buses, making them better on rougher or more remote roads. School buses can be either the standard "dog-nosed" type, with the engine out in front; or the "flat nose" type, with the engine either in front or at the rear. The location of the engine will affect how noisy the vehicle will be on the road, how much floor space is inside, where you can locate any underfloor storage compartments or water tanks, and how easy it will be to maintain. The location of the wheel wells can also vary, affecting ground clearance and your floorplan.

- **City Transit Buses:**

  Typically, these are buses that have been retired from use in a public transportation network. They sit low to the ground and have relatively high ceilings inside. The biggest drawback is that they are not very fuel-efficient over long distances, as they are designed for slow, stop-and-go traffic in urban settings. When bought used, they typically range in price from $5,000 to $15,000.

- **Intercity Motorcoaches:**

  While these may cost twice as much used as a transit bus, these vehicles, which are often function as charter or tour buses, are designed to be driven over long distances. They can be a good fit for those with more cash to spend. A number of companies offer high-end professional conversions. The biggest advantages are that they offer a more comfortable ride compared to other bus types and they have extra storage built into bays underneath the bus. One drawback is that, unlike school buses, they are not made to be driven on rough or bumpy roads.

- **Shuttle Buses:**

  Also called minibuses, microbuses, or

The old transit bus that Scott and Emily Manning revamped into a new home.

minicoaches, these vehicles are often seen running on continuous routes at airports, hospitals, assisted living facilities, churches, and school campuses. That means they can rack up a lot of mileage. Shuttle buses with diesel engines will last twice as long as gas-powered ones. Windows are relatively large, and some will be equipped with wheelchair lifts. If you intend to use the lift, make sure it is in working order prior to purchase.

Whichever type of bus you choose, Justine Meccio (We Got Schooled, page 24) has this tip: "Find out everything you can about that particular make and model, its engine and transmission, including common problems other owners have experienced with it." (See Resources, page 231 to start your research.)

Where to Buy a Bus

There are an estimated 480,000 school buses on the road in the United States, compared to only 67,000 transit buses—meaning that a retired school bus will be much easier to find than an old transit bus.

To buy a school bus, you can go directly to a school district and ask if they have surplus buses for sale. Police auctions and government surplus sales are potential resources as well. You cut out the middle man when you buy direct from these sources, meaning you'll get more for less, compared to going to a dealership for used vehicles.

It's vital to hire a competent professional—preferably a certified diesel mechanic who knows their way around large vehicles like buses and trucks—to inspect the entire bus prior to purchase. Ask to see the vehicle's maintenance service record, if available. For future reference, see if you can track down the manufacturer's service manual as well. With any well-used vehicle, it's likely that you will need to make repairs to your bus. Be sure to factor these repair costs into your budget.

Pre-Purchase Checklist

- Signs of rust
- Signs of a leaky roof
- Condition of the tires (these can be much more expensive to replace than on a car)
- Check the engine oil, transmission
- Check to see all lights, doors, windows, wheelchair lifts, wipers work
- Look under the bus to check for any signs of corrosion, wear or recent repairs
- Determine the kind of brakes it has (air brakes or hydraulic)
- Test drive

Finding a Location to Build and Store Your Bus

Once you have found a bus, you will need a location to park it while you work out things like vehicle registration and insurance. Ideally, this will be the same location where you can complete the build-out itself. If you live in a city, finding a suitable location may be more difficult, as local regulations may have stringent rules about where you can park a bus. Some bus owners rent storage facilities; others ask friends or family for access to a temporary parking spot.

Preliminary Design and Layout

Even prior to purchasing a bus, you can get started with the broader design process. To begin, ask yourself some very general questions. The answers you come up with will determine how you go about the conversion:

- What are your needs?
- How many people will be occupying the bus home?
- How will it be used and how often?
- What's your "wish list" (e.g., solar power system)?
- What kind of appliances do you need, or can live without?
- What about waste management (e.g., composting toilet or . . .)?
- How much water capacity do you plan to include in your freshwater and gray water tanks? What kind of water pump, if any? What about a water heater if you want hot water?
- How much electricity will be needed to power your home? Do you plan to be connected to the main power grid, or are you planning to "boondock" or "dry camp" off the main grid, or both? (In other words, will you need your own source of power?)
- Do you want a gas or diesel vehicle? If you choose diesel, do you want to convert it to run on more environmentally friendly biodiesel like waste vegetable oil (WVO)?

As you can see, there is a lot to research and consider even before buying a vehicle. After working through your list of needs and possibilities, and if you have an idea of what length and type of bus you are looking for, you can start sketching out some rough design layouts using those criteria. Keep in mind you will most likely have to account for the wheel wells (the semi-circular protrusions coming out of the bus floor) in your design. You can incorporate them into your design by placing seating or storage over them.

Once you have some rough layouts, you can refine them further on graph paper. Even better, you can use free 3D modeling software like Google's SketchUp to move things around on the screen. Generally speaking, the more planning you do before you start work, the more efficient and cost effective your conversion.

Purging Nonessential Belongings

If you are looking to move into a bus conversion full-time, then you may need to get rid of a lot of possessions you will no longer need. This can be a challenging task in and of itself, especially in a society where our cultural tendency is to find identity and validation through our belongings. The process of getting rid of unnecessary stuff can be liberating, and many people begin doing this simultaneous to the design and building process.

Here are some helpful rules of thumb. Sort your things into three piles: one for essential or sentimental things you must absolutely keep, one for things to be donated or given away, and one for things that will be discarded. To make this task easier, give away or discard anything you have not used in the past year—this goes for clothes, shoes, toys, electronics, and so on. The idea is to pare down your possessions to the items you actually need, use, and enjoy. This can be a daunting process, but there's a good reason to purge. "Be brutal," says Andrew Cleverley. "Minimizing your belongings will mean you won't need as much storage space, which will give you more living space."

When that first purge is all done, you will be surprised at how much lighter—literally and figuratively—you will feel. You may need to purge another time or two, or more. Once you get the hang of it, it'll become second nature when confronted with a potential purchase to ask yourself, "Do I really need this item? Will it fit in my small home?" Yet another tip for keeping a small space uncluttered is the "one in, one out" rule: When a new item is introduced into the home, another item must be given away or discarded.

DESIGN, LAYOUT, AND CONSTRUC-TION

Doing It Yourself

There's no doubt that you can save a lot of money if you build your bus conversion yourself. The alternative is to hire a contractor or motorhome conversion company, which can be more expensive. Of course, taking on such a project can present a huge challenge and quite a steep learning curve, especially if you have no experience handling power tools or don't have a basic knowledge about materials or how things are constructed. But the magic of living in the Information Age is that the knowledge is out there—be it online through video tutorials, forums, or websites, or from a book or an in-person workshop. With a bit of time, effort, and perseverance, you can learn how to do the work yourself. Of course, you can also hire out the trickier things you'd really rather not do, such as installing the electrical, propane, solar, or plumbing systems.

"The most challenging—and reward-ing—thing was learning how to accom-

Previous page:
The We Got Schooled bus, prior to conversion. "Blocking out the layout with masking tape and cardboard before we started building really helped us to tweak the design without wasting materials," says Justine Meccio.

This page:
Removing seats on Big Bertha with an angle grinder.

plish each step," says Starla Sullivan. "We had no experience doing anything construction related and supplies on the market are meant for building orthodox structures like houses. We not only had to teach ourselves construction, carpentry, plumbing, electrical, and more, we also needed to get creative with how we were going to do these things in a vehicle where nothing is level, nothing is square, everything flexes, and where building materials were not designed to be used."

Kyle Volkman adds this observation: "Since you can never count on the walls and floors of an old bus to be square or plumb, everything you build inside needs to be built off everything else, using screws to withstand movement and road vibration."

Ultimately, the conversion process is about discovering your hidden talents, your unique creative groove, and working with whatever skills and materials you may have.

"Be forgiving with yourself during the process," advises Justine Meccio. "Accept that things won't always go according to plan, that there will be mistakes, and that many things will probably take longer than expected. Perseverance, dedication, and continuing to make progress—no matter how incremental it seems—is what will get it finished."

Demolition

Safety first: Before beginning any construction work, make sure you have all the necessary safety gear. Be sure to wear eye and ear protection when cutting materials, and put on masks during sanding or when using chemicals.

Once you have found your bus, you can begin the process of removing the seats, racks, and other interior hardware you don't want. You will need some tools to do this, and you'll do yourself a big favor if you can get a buddy to help. Some DIYers suggest using hand ratchets and wrenches, but sometimes it will

be too difficult to budge the fasteners with these tools. If so, you can use an air compressor and an air-driven ratchet or impact gun. For an even quicker method, you can use an angle grinder to cut off bolts and fasteners. Make sure to use eye and ear protection when doing this, and be sure to sand all the protruding bits right down to the floor. If you are not using the bus's original heater or air-conditioning, then take them out at this stage.

Remove old flooring, paneling, ceilings, and old plywood and insulation, stripping everything down to the exterior metal. This will give you a good idea of any rust or damage that may have been hidden underneath. Patch and repair any holes you find. You can remove any rust by grinding it off with the angle grinder and/or covering it with rust converter, then painting it over with a rust-proofing product. Clean the inside and outside of the bus thoroughly.

Removal of old flooring down to the metal, and preparation for a new coat of paint.

Use masking tape to mark out full-scale dimensions of cabinets and furnishings on the bus.

Lay Out Your Design in Full-Scale

Once the bus is empty, you can do a real-life, full-scale mock-up of your planned layout. Use masking tape to mark out on the floor of the bus the dimensions of your seating, kitchen, bathroom, and bedroom. Determine if there are any windows you want to cover up; for example, for placement of a bathroom or closet. If doing so, the windows can be covered with a sheet of plywood, or even better, with some rigid insulation, cut to fit the window and placed on the interior. On the bus's exterior, you can affix a sheet of aluminum or steel over these windows.

Before you begin any more work, walk around and figure out whether your layout feels spacious or ergonomic enough. Consider how the layout flows when you walk from one area to another—does it feel efficient and is there enough room? Revise the design as needed.

"In doing a real-life mock-up, we quickly realized that we'd have way too little space to move around and just wouldn't be comfortable," says Justine. "We greatly simplified our plan—choosing to sacrifice storage and furniture features in exchange for a more open area."

Raising the Roof?

Elevating the roof on the bus is something to consider if you want to add more headspace inside. You must determine how this modification will affect the structural integrity of the bus, as buses are designed to stay in one piece in the event of a roll-over accident. So raising the roof—essentially cutting a part or all of the roof, inserting spacers, and then reattaching everything—should be done with professional help. It will add to the cost and time needed to complete the conversion, and it will add to the annual cost of heating and cooling the interior.

Flooring

Once everything has been stripped down, it's time to add insulation and then the subfloor, using at least 1/2" plywood. Insulating your floor is a good idea if you plan to spend any time in cold or hot climates; you will save money on heating and cooling the interior. A significant amount of heat can transfer out to the exterior through uninsulated floors, and cold, drafty floors are not comfortable, to say the least. There is a variety of possibilities, so it's a good idea to research what kind of insulating materials and R-values offer the most value and are the most efficient for your situation. (R-values are a measure of the resistance of a material to heat flow—the higher the number, the more insulating the material is.)

Framing

Next up is framing out any walls, closets, cabinets, appliances, water tanks (consider three types: freshwater; gray water, which is wastewater from showers, sinks, and laundry; and black water, which is from the toilet), seat-

Opposite page: Raising the roof on the Thompson bus.

This page: Framing out the children's bunk beds on the Trebitowskis' bus, Blue Steel.

Starla Sullivan, using a contoured template of the roofline to mark out cuts in the wood paneling.

ing, platforms, and so on. You can use standard-size, dimensional lumber (for example, 2 × 4 or 2 × 6). Alternatively, you can use metal stud framing, which is more lightweight but also more expensive. Remember the handy rule of "measure twice, because you can only cut once!"

It's also a good idea to create a contoured template of the curvature of the bus's roofline. This template will help you make sure the partitions and cabinetry consistently line up with the bus's curved roofline. Be sure to mark the locations of any pipes or systems that require openings through the walls and ceiling, such as those for plumbing and ceiling vents.

You will need to devise a system to fasten things such as framing or cladding to the bus's ceiling. Some methods to achieve this include using metal brackets that screw directly to the bus's metal framework, or using wooden furring strips that serve as an in-between layer.

Materials

There are many possibilities when it comes to sourcing and choosing materials for your conversion. Try to choose eco-friendly materials, including paints low in volatile organic compounds (VOCs), whenever possible. They will not off-gas toxins and will therefore contribute to an indoor air quality that's healthier to breathe.

Besides using new and conventional lumber and hardware, consider using salvaged materials, reclaimed fixtures, and secondhand appliances. Not only will you save money, but you can add a bit of extra charm to your home. "Purchasing all of your wood at the big box stores can get expensive fast and doesn't add much character," says Zack Andrews. "Look for wood at Habitat for Humanity ReStores, offcuts or extras from construction workshops and individual contractors, or, if you have land available, use a sawmill to make your own."

Electrical and Plumbing

If you are unsure about electrical and plumbing systems and how to install them, take the time to consult print manuals, online resources, and forums. Alternatively, to really make sure it's done right, hire an electrician and/or plumber to do the job.

To begin the process, figure out where you would like to have your light switches, outlets, and electrical boxes and then mount them. Run the wiring throughout the bus. Remember to check your local building codes for any requirements. If you are planning to put in a solar power system, determine your electrical usage needs and then size your system accordingly.

Size up what your water system might look like. After establishing the preliminary estimates of your water usage and the size of your water tank(s), you need to figure out where to place them. If you plan to live or travel in colder climates, make sure to insulate your water tank(s) and plumbing lines. Your goal should be to design and install a water system that won't freeze up during the winter. Placing

Above: Using metal brackets to attach wood framing to the metal ribs of Big Bertha.

Right: Wood siding is attached to wooden furring strips, which are in turn attached to the metal ribs on the roof of Zack Andrews and Annie King's bus, Stormy.

the tank(s) somewhere within the insulated interior of the bus is a good way to do this. Convenient hiding places include the spaces under benches, couches, and beds.

For more details, see the section in this chapter: Plumbing, Heating, Cooling, Ventilation, and Power (page 219).

Insulation

Insulating your bus is a good idea, even if you don't plan to venture into colder climates. Insulation is the best way to make a living space more energy efficient to heat and cool—whether it's a conventionally built house or a vehicle conversion. Depending on the material used, the insulation will also help keep the interior from becoming damp and will soundproof your bus somewhat.

There are many different kinds of insulating materials out there. You can use spray foam, rigid foam insulations, and fiberglass batt insulation. More eco-friendly insulation options include cork, cellulose, recycled cotton and wool, and aerogel. It's worth considering a more eco-friendly insulation because these alternatives will help you achieve better indoor air quality, as they off-gas less toxins than insulation made with chemicals or petroleum derivatives.

Walls and Ceilings

After insulating the wall cavities and ceiling of your bus, it's time to cover them up. Once again, you have lots of material choices and options. What you choose will depend on your budget and the aesthetic you want to achieve. For walls, some bus converters stick with drywall. Others use plywood sheets, tongue-and-groove siding, or another engineered wood product. For ceilings, you'll need a material that can flex and follow the curvature of the roof. Adding a layer of furring strips underneath first is a good idea, as this gives the ceiling material something to attach to. To finish off the look and to hide uneven corners and joints between the walls, floor, doors, windows, and ceiling, you can use decorative trim or molding.

Furniture (the Transforming Kind)

Space is limited on a bus, so it's a big priority to find ways to maximize it. Making multifunctional furniture is one way to do this, and "transformer" furnishings are a recurring theme in many small spaces, bus conversions included. Here are some basic strategies to make your furniture or living spaces do double duty:

- Create hidden storage wherever you can (examples: built-in storage under couches, ottomans, beds, platforms, and even under the floor itself, using trapdoors)
- Add overhead shelving
- Install a fold-down table or a portable, foldable table
- If you have raised the roof of your bus, add a loft for extra space
- The living room couch can be designed to fold out to become a guest bed

Spray foam insulation for
Big Bertha.

- Include a hinged bed (also called a Murphy bed) that can be folded up or pushed away to free up extra space as needed

Fixtures and Appliances

When choosing fixtures and appliances, try to find items that are energy- and resource-efficient. For example, to conserve water, install low-flow faucets and shower heads. For lighting fixtures, energy-efficient LED lights shine brightly and use very little electricity. It is also a good idea to find appliances that combine more than one function into the same machine—for instance, you can install a combination washer and dryer, or a microwave that also functions as a convection oven.

For refrigeration, you have a number of choices. What you select depends on your power source and needs. You can choose a refrigerator that's fueled by propane, or one that uses electricity, or one that can run on a variety of power sources. You can also consider using an icebox or converting a small chest freezer into an energy-efficient refrigerator (as seen on Zack Andrews and Annie King's bus). There are many tutorials online that show you how to do this conversion. The drawback is that you can't use it for freezing, only refrigeration. But a converted freezer ends up using much less energy than a regular refrigerator, as chest freezers are already super-insulated to begin with.

You have several choices for stoves. You could use a propane-fueled stove (using this stove, however, will create some interior condensation), or you could use a portable induction stove that uses electricity if you have access to the main electrical grid or use a solar power system. You can even use a camping stove.

To save money, use secondhand appliances, which can be found in RV salvage yards, some thrift stores, or through the classified ads.

Bathrooms

In designing the bathroom, you may decide to add a tub in addition to a shower. For a unique touch, you can use reclaimed items like a large watertight container (such as the metal horse trough used by the Sullivans in their bus). To convert it into a tub, you simply drill a drain hole in the bottom and connect it to your plumbing system.

For the toilet, there are many possible options, depending on your needs. It can range from the traditional flush toilet (meaning you would need access to a sewage hookup at all times) or something more suited for off-grid applications. Options include an RV-type toilet that flushes into a black water holding tank, a portable camping toilet, or a waterless, dry toilet such as a composting toilet. Composting toilets use little to no water and can either be custom built or bought from a manufacturer. When done right, the composting process will transform human excreta into nutrient-rich fertilizer, which can then be used to nourish non-edible plants.

Plumbing, Heating, Cooling, Ventilation, and Power

Plumbing

As mentioned elsewhere in this book, water conservation is essential when living in a vehicle conversion. If you're not connected to a water main, you only have as much freshwater as you can carry with you, which means using water as frugally as possible to maximize the time you have before you need to refill the tank. Many tiny home homeowners notice that they are much more aware and conscientious about water use when they are living off the grid, and how much water can be wasted when it isn't treated like the precious resource it really is.

Consider how much water you think you will need in your home. Will you be taking lots of showers and washing your family's clothes? Or will you just need enough for drinking and washing dishes? Do you plan to reuse the water from washing dishes, clothes, and showers (i.e., gray water) for watering plants—if you do, how will you store, filter, or divert it? Determine your unique needs and configure your plumbing system to meet these estimates.

Another question to ponder is whether you will need an electrical water pump for your home, or if a foot-powered pump will suffice. You might want to combine both into your system, as Kyle Volkman did in his Yetibus conversion. By combining an RV water pump with a foot-operated pump, Kyle's water system works even when there's no electricity.

Heating

There are four main options for heating in a bus conversion: propane, wood, electric, and diesel. In order to select the heater that's appropriate for your space, it may also help to use a heat loss calculator (see Resources, page 231).

Propane is cheap and readily available to purchase almost anywhere in metal tanks, and can be used for heating, hot water, and cooking. Propane-based heaters can be portable standalone units, or they can be more permanently installed and vented to the outside. One of the big drawbacks is the tendency for condensation to form on interior surfaces and windows when using propane to heat your home. Propane is a combustible fuel, so there are precautions to take. If using propane on your bus, it is a good idea to crack a window open and install a combustible gas detector to alert you if there's ever a leak. You should test and replace the detector batteries on a regular basis.

A woodstove will create a drier heat and is a better choice if you plan to stay in wet, cold climates. Many high-efficiency woodstoves are now available that are specifically designed for small spaces. They use very little wood to quickly heat up a small space. Installing a woodstove means installing a stovepipe as well, and finding space to store your fuel—wood, charcoal, peat, and so on. Once again, as a safety precaution, make sure to install a carbon monoxide detector to alert you if there are any problems with the woodstove's venting system.

Electric heaters are a good option if you are going to have access to a main power grid most of the time or if you have a solar power system. A small electric space heater can be sufficient to heat a small space and can be used in conjunction with another type of heating, such as propane (as Justine Meccio and Ryan Ayers have done on their bus).

If your bus is already running on **diesel**, you can purchase a diesel air heater and install it using a conversion kit. This allows you to tap into your existing diesel fuel tank and heat the interior using a highly efficient drip system.

Cooling

One of the best ways to make sure the interior temperature of your bus stays comfortable year-round without expending too much energy is to insulate it well.

Beyond that, to help stay cool, install an air conditioner. You can use one that's specifically designed for RV use or you can use a portable unit.

If you have solar panels and plan to have your bus parked most of the time, consider making the panels detachable. This way, you can park your bus in the shade to keep the interior cool, and then connect your solar panels nearby in the sun (perhaps on movable frames).

Ventilation

In a small, enclosed space such as a bus, good ventilation is a must. Installing a roof vent is therefore a good idea. There are many different designs out there, depending on what kind of features you desire. Options include adjustable speed fans that can draw air both in and out. Some even have sensors that can alert you if it's raining. When installing appliances that need venting to the outside, make sure you follow the manufacturer's instructions for correct installation and setup.

Power

If you want to travel around with some modern conveniences at your disposal, an off-grid renewable energy source is the way to go. Solar panels mounted on the roof can power everyday electrical conveniences like lights, a refrigerator, electric cooktops, fans, and other gadgets while on the road.

Solar technology is improving at a rapid pace and costs have decreased dramatically in recent years, making it an affordable and convenient option. Do-it-yourself solar panel installation kits are available and will help you save money as well. To correctly size your solar power system, you will need to estimate your electrical usage (see Resources on page 231 for some handy calculators). Using energy-efficient appliances is a plus.

There's so much information out there on solar power systems that it's worth a deep dive into books and websites to find out what you need to know so that you can do the job yourself. But of course, if you have the extra money to spend, you can hire a professional to design and install a solar power system for you.

Exterior Paint

You can take your bus to be professionally painted at an auto body shop or an RV repair shop, but this will cost you. To save money, paint it yourself. First wash it down well (a pressure washer will come in handy here) and rehabilitate any rusty spots. Sanding down the entire exterior (and not just the rusty areas) will help the new coats of paint adhere better. Any areas with bare metal should be primed with rust-proof paint. Remove any hardware that you don't want painted (such as plates and reflectors). Keep in mind that in most states it's illegal to impersonate a school bus, meaning that all previous insignia, flashers, and stop signs must be removed, especially if you intend to register it as a recreational vehicle.

There's a range of paint options to choose from, from the more expensive

Top: Roof vent on Stormy the bus.

Bottom: Justine Meccio removing the lettering from the We Got Schooled bus.

automotive paints to the more afford-able "poor man's automotive paint." This cheaper version of automotive paint involves using urethane-based paint for marine and industrial applications that's custom mixed with a hardener (as Justine Meccio and Ryan Ayers did on their bus). Paint can be either rolled on by hand with a roller brush or sprayed on with an airless sprayer for a more even finish.

There's a rainbow of colors to choose from. A lighter color for the bus's exterior means more sunlight (and therefore more heat) will be reflected away—which will help keep the bus cooler. You can play around with different colors for the trim around the windows, or add decorative elements like stripes, patterning, or lettering. Make sure to use masking tape for a cleaner-looking paint job.

Converting Your Bus to Run on Biodiesel
Traveling around in a big vehicle such as a bus can consume a lot of fuel—and therefore a lot of money. It also doesn't help that buses aren't built with fuel economy in mind. One way to minimize a bus's environmental impact is to convert it to run on biodiesel—vegetable- or animal fat-based oil sourced from restaurants that discard it as a waste product. This waste oil is put through a chemical process that transforms it into a nontoxic liquid with lower viscosity, which is then used as fuel. Biodiesel has many positive qualities: it produces less harmful emissions than petroleum-based fuels, it helps the engine run cleaner and smoother, and it saves money in the long run. On the other hand, biodiesel may have lower performance in colder weather, and the up-front costs are higher.

In any case, if you are considering going a bit "greener" with your bus, converting it to run on biodiesel may be the way to go. There are many resources available online and elsewhere that can point you in the right direction.

TIPS FOR A HEALTHIER, MORE EFFICIENT HOME

Many of today's eco-friendly strategies are predicated on the common sense approach of "waste not, want not" that previous generations also held dear. Implementing these greener strategies may require a slightly higher investment of money or effort up front, but you can generally expect to recoup the investment over time due to increases in efficiency. For those intending to or already living the bus life, some application of eco-friendly strategies are necessary to make it more successful.

Freshwater

Freshwater storage represents one of the big limiting factors aboard a bus or any RV that moves around. Although installing a larger freshwater tank means you'll have more time between refills, your supply isn't unlimited (as it seems to be in a home that's hooked up to a municipal water system). Conservation is key. It's therefore important to be cognizant of your water consumption. Some tips: use low-flow faucets and shower heads, and in addition to an electric water pump, consider installing a foot-operated water pump (instead of an electrical one). The act of manually pumping your freshwater will remind you to conserve it.

Gray water and black water

Gray water refers to water that has been used for bathing and for washing clothes and dishes. Gray water has many uses, including flushing toilets or watering non-edible plants. To ensure that gray water does not harm plants, it's best to use biodegradable soaps, or products that are "plant-friendly"—no salts, boron, or chlorine bleach. Black water refers to water that contains fecal contamination, so it should not be reused. To limit how much black water you produce and to reduce your total water use, consider installing a composting toilet instead of a regular flush toilet.

Waste

Since there's no weekly waste pickup when you're aboard a bus, many bus homeowners find themselves reducing waste so that there's less to lug around. Some tips to reduce your waste: consume less; buy things in bulk, using your own reusable containers; choose items with the least amount of packaging whenever possible; and skip the plastic bag at the cashier. Most important, if your setup allows, compost organic matter.

Air

Any enclosed space will benefit from the addition of vents and fans of some sort. Healthy indoor air quality is essential to the well-being of the occupants of any home, and a bus conversion is no exception. To minimize the off-gassing of toxins into your indoor air, choose your materials, paints, and finishes carefully. Opt for items that are formaldehyde-free or low VOCs (volatile organic compounds).

Power

The cost of solar panels has decreased dramatically over the last several years, and they have become a popular option for those who want to make their home operate partially or completely off the grid. Battery technology is also improving, and it's becoming easier to store that free, renewable solar energy too. Being able to have all the modern comforts and electrical amenities—without needing to be tethered to the grid—is an alluring possibility that you can make into a reality.

REGISTRATION, LICENSING, AND INSURANCE

Planning to live full-time in a vehicle—even one converted into a well-designed home on wheels—can present some interesting challenges in terms of registration and insurance. Each state has different rules and regulations, and it's up to you to find out what they are. One common approach is to have your bus titled and insured as a motorhome, which means that you will need at least running water, a bed, and a toilet. It's a good idea to check out and ask questions on bus conversion websites or skoolie forums—these sources can be a big help for answering your questions.

For registration, you can start by going to your local Department of Motor Vehicles and having them walk you through the process. Even the answers you get at the Department of Motor Vehicles will vary, as it will depend on whom you talk to. As Scott Manning wryly puts it: "Hope and pray your state's not annoying and that the clerk you work with isn't having a bad day like ours was. For the first year we paid $1,200 because a clerk didn't know how to label the rig and ended up categorizing it for tax purposes as if it were Bon Jovi's $1.4 million tour bus. The following year they corrected it and paid us $700 back retrospectively after covering the next year's registration."

Keep in mind that a larger bus may also mean you will need to obtain a new type of license to drive it. License classes in most states are determined by gross vehicle weight rating (GVWR). This is the maximum operating weight of a vehicle, as specified by the manufacturer, and it includes the vehicle's chassis, body, engine, engine fluids, fuel, accessories, driver, passengers, and cargo. Overloading a vehicle past its GVWR can present a number of potential problems with safety, affecting things like braking or suspension. So it will be important for you to know the GVWR of your vehicle, and to check with your local DMV to determine if you will need another license to drive it, which will probably require you to pass a written or driving test.

Insurance will be easier (and cheaper) to obtain if the driver has a good driving record. Make sure the bus meets all local DMV requirements, and have proof on hand (such as photos) showing the bus has had all flashing lights, signs, and school insignia removed, and that it has an independent source of power, water, toilet, and bed. If you already have coverage with an insurance company for your home or car, ask your broker first if they can offer you insurance for your bus. If your company isn't able to insure your bus conversion, here is a list of insurance companies that might: State Farm, National General, Progressive, Farm Bureau, Liberty Mutual, Good Sam Club, and AIS.

It is a great idea to have a contingency plan in case your bus happens to break down in the middle of nowhere. You can sign up for a roadside assistance plan from agencies like the American Automobile Association (AAA), Coach-Net, and Good Sam Club. Such services are especially valuable if you plan to travel extensively.

PLACES
TO PARK

If you plan to stay put for long stretches of time, you could buy or rent land to park your bus conversion. Some of the bus homeowners profiled in this book have done just that. If you plan to roam around, campgrounds and RV parks are among some of the places where you can park your bus for extended periods of time. Fees for renting a spot to park your bus will vary from location to location. For overnight stays between destinations, you may find parking locations in rest areas, truck stops, and even some parking lots of big-box stores like Walmart, Sam's Club, Home Depot, and Lowe's. "My favorite place to park is on national forest land, either at free campsites with 14-day limits, or on abandoned logging roads," says Kyle Volkman. Parking a bus on city streets may be trickier. "If I'm going to be parked in a city, it can be a challenge doing so without prior arrangements, as it's usually against city parking ordinances to park a vehicle like a bus on the street. But it can be done, and can be as easy as having friends with driveway space, or seeking some driveway space on Craigslist and treating your bus like a self-contained auxiliary room in a rental situation."

Another bothersome issue concerning bus conversions is the public perception of them. There are some stereotypes due to their historic associations with the hippie counterculture. But as we've seen from the well-crafted house buses in this book, these are misperceptions. Nevertheless, it's something most bus homeowners will likely deal with. For instance, some RV parks may refuse you entry if they see you pull up in a conversion bus. One potential solution is to book your spot at an RV park via their website, if at all possible. There may still be issues when you arrive, but remember you are driving a motorhome (a conversion, yes, but still a motorhome nonetheless), and so you should insist that it be treated and referred to as such. Whatever happens, staying calm, level-headed, and polite can go a long way toward breaking barriers.

In general, while it may be best to stay incognito to avoid harassment from local residents or law enforcement, you may find that there are cases where you want to draw attention to yourself. Jeanine Pfeiffer, who teaches university courses on ethnoecology, says, "When parking in local neighborhoods, to become less of a suspicious enigma, I designed a tagline and logo saying 'Connecting Biological and Cultural Diversity,' with my website address. I printed it on magnetic signs that I affixed to both side walls. This way, people know who I am and can learn more about what I do."

As the possibilities for travel expand, so does our sense of what constitutes work and home. Is work something you show up to do at a designated place and time, day in and day out? Is home a static building with four walls and a foundation, for which you pay to have the privilege of sleeping in? Or could these cultural notions evolve into something else entirely?

It's difficult to say where these trends of mobility, remote work, minimalism, small-space living, and increasingly accessible travel will go. There's also no guarantee that such alternatives will solve the broader problems and policies behind growing income inequality and the current affordable housing crisis. But in the future, as digital nomadism and off-grid technologies catch on at a massive scale, might the conventional structures of home and neighborhood eventually develop into movable cities or rolling communities, as some think-ers and visionaries have hypothesized? Might people also be compelled to use their homes-on-wheels as a way to move around as increasingly severe weather events dictate, as some of the bus homeowners in this book have done in response to the historically unprecedented devastation wrought by wildfires and hurricanes? Could living the "bus life" remain as it has since the beginning—as a way to enable people to travel more leisurely with the comforts of home—or could it become a viable alternative for debt-free housing? Could it be both?

It's hard to say. What's certain is that more and more people are looking for alternatives that give them increased freedom and more opportunities to redefine what their dream lifestyle looks and feels like, so that they can live out those dreams on their own terms. And as the inspiring stories in these pages have shown, it may very well come on the wheels of a bus.

BUS CONVERSIONS

Buses101
www.buses101.com

Build A Green RV
"Heat Loss Calculator for
Camper Van Conversions"
www.buildagreenrv.com

**The School Bus
Conversion Network**
www.skoolie.net

YouTube.com
See Contributors, page 233, for
links to videos from some of the bus
homeowners featured in this book

DIY SOLAR AND ELECTRICITY

HandyBob's Blog
www.handybobsolar.wordpress.com

The Reckless Choice
"Handy Bob Solar Summary"
www.therecklesschoice.com/2017/
07/07/handy-bob-solar-summary

Solar Wind UK
www.solar-wind.co.uk/cable-sizing-
DC-cables.html

Wholesale Solar
"Off-Grid Calculator"
"Battery Bank Sizing Calculator"
www.wholesalesolar.com

MECHANICAL

Diesel Hub
www.dieselhub.com

DESIGN

TreeHugger
www.treehugger.com

Tiny House Swoon
www.tinyhouseswoon.com

Tiny House Talk
www.tinyhousetalk.com

The Tiny Life
www.thetinylife.com

Tiny House Design
www.tinyhousedesign.com

Tiny House Blog
www.tinyhouseblog.com

Pinterest
www.pinterest.com

RV AND NOMADIC LIFESTYLE

Technomadia
www.technomadia.com

Gone with the Wynns
www.gonewiththewynns.com

Wand'rly
https://wandrlymagazine.com

Campendium
www.campendium.com

Ultimate Campgrounds
www.ultimatecampgrounds.com

Allstays
www.allstays.com

SOCIAL MEDIA

Facebook groups:
Skoolie Converters
Skoolie Geeks

Reddit:
TinyHouses
vandwellers
DIY

BIBLIOGRAPHY

Belasco, Warren James. *Americans on the Road: From Autocamp to Motel, 1910–1945.* Johns Hopkins University Press, 1997.

Butterfield, Brock. "Picking the right source of heat for your bus conversion." Bus Life Adventure. www.buslifeadventure.com.

Eidt, Jack. "Communal Utopia: The Farm in Rural Tennessee." *WilderUtopia* (blog), April 24, 2016, www.wilderutopia.com.

Freelancers Union & eLance-oDesk. "Freelancing in America: A National Survey of the New Workforce." 2014, https://blog.freelancersunion.org.

Helmore, Edward. "How Ken Kesey's LSD-fuelled bus trip created the psychedelic 60s." *The Guardian,* August 6, 2011, www.theguardian.com.

Kusisto, Laura. "Many Who Lost Homes to Foreclosure in Last Decade Won't Return—NAR." *The Wall Street Journal,* April 20, 2015, www.wsj.com.

MacKechnie, Christopher. "What Happens to Buses After Their Useful Life is Over?" ThoughtCo, May 17, 2017, www.thoughtco.com.

McClure, Louis C., and Ben Rosander. *How to Build Low Cost Motorhomes.* Ben Rosander, 2004.

Mitchell, Ryan. *Tiny House Living: Ideas for Building and Living Well in Less than 400 Square Feet.* Betterway Home, 2014.

Perry, Mark J. "New US homes today are 1,000 square feet larger than in 1973 and living space per person has nearly doubled." *AEIdeas* (blog), June 5, 2016, www.aei.org/publication/blog.

Plachno, Larry. *Beginner's Guide to Converted Coaches.* Transportation Trails, 1992.

Rosander, Ben. *Select and Convert Your Bus into a Motorhome on a Shoestring.* Ben Rosander, 2002.

Tomasso, Linda Powers. "A Study of Sustainability at RV Parks." Program in Sustainability & Environmental Management, Harvard University Extension School, December 13, 2010, www.eplerwood.com/beta/images/Tomasso%20Grad%20Project_RV%20park%20sustainability_2010_XII.pdf.

Trant, Kate. *Home Away from Home: The World of Camper Vans and Motorhomes.* Black Dog, 2005.

Twitchell, James B. *Winnebago Nation: The RV in American Culture.* Columbia University Press, 2014.

Wathen, Jordan. "Here's the Size of the Average American's Mortgage." The Motley Fool, February 25, 2017, www.fool.com.

A huge thank you to everyone who contributed to this book for sharing their inspiring stories, far-seeing insights, and helpful tips—and for showing that another way is indeed possible.

WE GOT SCHOOLED
Justine Meccio and Ryan Ayers
www.wegotschooled.com

NATURAL STATE NOMADS
Zack Andrews and Annie King
www.naturalstatenomads.com
Facebook: naturalstatenomads
Instagram: naturalstatenomads

TREBVENTURE
Brandon and Ashley Trebitowski
www.trebventure.com
Instagram: trebventure

ADVENTURE OR BUST
Brittany and Steven Altmann
www.adventureorbust.com

BIG BERTHA
Brian and Starla Sullivan
Facebook: schoolbuslife
Instagram: schoolbuslife
Patreon: berthatv

WHERE WE ROAM
Scott and Emily Manning
www.whereweroam.com
Instagram: familyonabus

BUS LIFE NZ
Andrew Cleverley and
Amber Mackintosh
Facebook: buslifenz
Instagram: buslifenz
Patreon: buslifenz
Youtube: buslifenz

VON THOMPSON CREATIVE
Jeremy and Mira Thompson
www.vonthompsoncreative.com

THE CHAMPION
Jeanine Pfeiffer
www.jeaninepfeiffer.com
Facebook: JeaninePfeiffer
Instagram: dr_pfeiffer
LinkedIn: jeaninepfeiffer
Twitter: JeaninePfeiffer

THE MIDWEST WANDERERS
Luke and Rachel Davis
www.midwestwanderers.com

THE YETIBUS
Kyle Volkman
www.kylevolkman.com
www.nomadicustoms.com
Instagram:
kylevolkman, nomadicustoms
Tumblr: thewanderingyeti

THE QUEEN OF PEACE
Charles Kern (left)
www.artbuildersguild.com
Instagram: lookatthatbus

Pages 7, 22, 41–51, 192, 194, 208, 214 (right), 221 (top), 233 (middle): Natural State Nomads; page 10: Tomas Quinones, 2012; page 11: Anne Deschaine; page 14 (top): Library of Congress, Prints & Photographs Division, LC-DIG-ggbain-19778; page 14 (bottom): State Archives of Florida; page 16: Joe Mabel; pages 25–37, 203, 221 (bottom), 222, 233 (top): Justine Meccio Photography; pages 53–63, 198, 211, 233 (bottom): Trebventure; pages 65–75: Catch A Star Fine Art Photography; pages 77–89, 234 (middle left): Scott & Emily; pages 91–109, 210, 234 (bottom left): Von Thompson Creative; pages 111–123, 204–207, 212, 214 (left), 216–217, 234 (top right): Bertha TV; pages 125–133, 234 (middle right): Bus Life NZ; pages 135–145, 234 (bottom right): Jeanine Pfeiffer; pages 147–159, 235 (top): The Midwest Wanderers; pages 161–173, 235 (middle): Kyle Volkman; pages 175–191, 235 (bottom): Charles Kern; page 234 (top left): Mandy Lea Photo. Endpapers: Kyle Volkman.

A

Adventure or Bust (Altmann, Brittany and Steven), 64–75
  tips and features, 67
Adventure or Bust (blog), 66
Air, 225
AIS, 227
Altmann, Brittany and Steven, bus conversion of, 64–75, 234
Altmann, Hannah, 69
American Automobile Association (AAA), 227
American Motor Bus Company, 15
Americans on the Road: From Autocamp to Motel, 1910-1945 (Belasco), 14–15
Andrews, Zack, bus conversion of, with King, Annie, 38–51, 233
Appliances, 26, 42, 44, 45, 58, 67, 114, 165, 218
  buying from salvage yards, 149
  DIY conversions of, 42, 45
Art Builders Guild, 176
Auto-camping, 14, 15
Automotive paints, 222–223
Ayers, Ryan, bus conversion of, with Meccio, Justine, 24–37, 223

B

Bathrooms, 13, 30, 33, 42, 47, 59, 117, 218
  showers in, 30, 33, 47, 59, 73
  shower-tub in, 156
  toilets in, 30. 47, 33, 42, 67, 73, 86, 102, 117, 127, 156
Battery technology, 225
Bedrooms, 34–35, 48, 74, 83–85, 95, 105, 121, 132–133, 137, 143–145, 170, 181

children's, 61, 88–89
loft, 96–98, 157–158
master, 62
Beds
  bunk, 61
  Murphy, 79, 84, 177, 181, 216
  platform, 120, 166
  queen-size, 35, 74
  single, 118–119
Belasco, Warren, 14–15
Belongings, purging nonessential, 201
Big Bertha (Sullivan, Brian and Starla), 110–123
  tips and features, 114
Big-box stores, 229
Biodiesel fuel, 20
  converting bus to run on, 223
Black water, 165, 225
Blogs
  Adventure or Bust, 66
  We Got Schooled, 26
"Blue Steel," 54, *57*
Bon Jovi, tour bus of, 227
Bookcases, 29
Boondock, 148
Building a Bus Cottage and Mini-bus RV (Thompson, Jeremy and Mira), 90–109
Bunk beds, 61
Bus conversions
  appliances for, 26, 42, 44, 45, 58, 67, 114, 165, 218
  bathrooms for, 13, 30, 33, 42, 47, 59, 117, 218
  bedrooms in, 34–35, 48, 74, 83–85, 95, 105, 121, 132–133, 137, 143–145, 170, 181
  cooling for, 67, 139, 220
  exterior paint for, 221–223

fixtures for, 218
furniture for, 215, 218
heating for, 139, 219–220
hippie counterculture and, 15, 17
history of, 13–15, 14–15
living space in, 28, 30, 43, 56, 68–69, 81, 115, 127, 128–130, 142, 154–155, 178
plumbing for, 219
power for, 220–221
public perception of, 229
purging nonessential belongings, 201
ventilation for, 220
Buses
  buying, 199
  choosing, 196
  converting to run on biodiesel, 223
  costs to convert, 13
  finding location to build and store, 200
  places to park your, 41, 182–183, 229–230
  preliminary design and layout, 13, 20, 26, 40, 54, 69, 78–79, 81, 92, 114, 149, 162, 176, 200
  pre-purchase checklist, 200
  renovations from scratch, 18–19
  sizes of, 196–197
  types of, 8, 197–199
Bus life
  choosing, 8–9
  environmental impact of, 19–20
By the Grace of the Queen of Peace (Kern, Charles), 174–191, 235
  tips and features, 177

C

Campgrounds, 229
Camping culture, history of, 13–15
Carbon-neutral lifestyle, 139, 140
The Champion (Pfeiffer, Jeanine), 134–145
City buses, 8, 197
Cleverley, Andrew, 124–133, 201, 234
Coach buses, 8
Coach-Net, 227
Compost, 67, 73
Conklin, Roland R., 15
    family bus of, 14
Conservation, 224–225
Cooling, 139, 220
    costs of, 67
Cottage-style workshop, 108–109
Coworking space, 17–18

D

Davis, Luke and Rachel, bus conversion of, 148–149, 235
"Dead spaces," 42
Dehumidifier, 114
Developing Apps and Homeschooling on a Bus (Trebitowski, Ashley and Brandon)
    tips and features, 56
Digital nomad movement, 9, 17–18, 230
Dinettes, 169
DIY conversions, 18, 20, 40, 42, 45, 54
Dogs, sleeping space for, 74
Domestic tourism, 15
Driver's seat, 171, 179

E

Eco-friendliness, 17, 112, 224–225
Edison, Thomas, 15

Electrical system setup, electrician check of, 54
Electric heaters, 139, 219
Emergency exit, 35, 71
Escapees, 20–21
Exterior paint, 26, 37, 221–223

F

The Farm, 17
Farm Bureau, 227
Firestone, Harvey, 15
Fixtures, 218
Floor plan
    keeping open, 165
Ford, Henry, 15
Ford Model T, 14
Foreclosure, 9
Freelance economy, 17–18, 27
Freshwater, 30, 54, 156, 224–225
Furniture, 99, 215–218. See also Beds
Further, 16–17

G

Gaskin, Stephen, 17
Global recession, 9
Good Sam Club, 227
Google's SketchUp, 201
Gray water, 54, 67
Great Recession, 18
Grey water, 225
Gross vehicle weight rating (GVWR), 227
"Gypsy Van," 15
Gypsy wagons, 14

H

"Harriet," 14
Heating, 139, 219–220
    costs of, 67

electric heater, 139, 219
    potbellied stove for, 155
    propane, 57, 114, 116, 141, 219
    woodstove, 42, 46, 99, 165, 169, 190, 219–220
Hippie culture, 66, 229
    bus conversions and, 15, 17
Home, tips for healthier, more efficient, 224–225
Home Away From Home: The World of Camper Vans and Motorhomes (Trant), 15
Home Depot, 229
Home offices, 87, 122
Household, size of average, 12
Housing bubble, collapse of, 9
Housing market, crash of, 9

I

Induction stovetops, 114, 116
Insulation, 67
Insurance, 227
Intercity motorcoaches, 197
International Code Council (ICC), 13
International residential building code, 13
Internet, 8, 17, 54
Interstate highway development, 15

K

Kern, Charles, 174–191, 235
Kesey, Ken, 15, 16, 17
King, Annie, bus conversion of, with Andrews, Zack, 38–51, 233
Kitchens, 27, 30, 32, 42, 44–45, 55, 58, 65, 70–72, 82, 100–101,

116, 131, 150–153, 164, 167, 180, 184–185, 187, 189
    appliances in, 26, 42, 44, 45, 58, 67, 114, 153, 165, 218

L

LED lighting, 165
Liberty Mutual, 227
License, 227
    classes of, 227
Living Life to the Fullest (Cleverley, Andrew and Amber), 124–133, 201, 234
    tips and features, 127
Living space, 28, 30, 43, 56, 68–69, 81, 115, 127, 128–130, 142, 154–155, 178
Location independence, 18
Loft bedrooms, 96–98, 157–158
Lowe's, 229

M

Mackintosh, Amber, 126, 234
Manning, Emily and Scott, bus conversion of, 76–89, 227
Meccio, Justine, bus conversion of, with Ayers, Ryan, 24–37, 223
Merry Panksters, 15, 66
Microbuses, 197
The Midwest Wanderers (Davis, Luke and Rachel), 146–159, 235
    tips and features, 149
Minibuses, 197
Minicoaches, 199
"Minnette," 90–109
Mortgages, 12–13
Multifunctionality, 120
Murphy beds, 79, 84, 177, 181, 216

N

National General, 227
Natural State Nomads (Andrews, Zack, and King, Annie), 38–51
    tips and features, 42
Nooks, 94, 157

O

Offgrid technology, 230
"One in, one-out" rule, 201

P

Petroleum-based fuels, 223
Pfeiffer, Jeanine, bus conversion of, 134–145, 229, 234
Plants, 30
Plumbing, 219. See also Bathrooms; Kitchens
Portable crane, 36
Potbellied stove, 155
Power, 220–221, 225
    solar, 8, 26, 40, 42, 49, 54, 57, 159, 165, 225
The Professor and Her Champion (Pfeiffer, Jeanine), 134–145, 229, 234
    tips and features, 141
Progressive, 227
Propane, 57, 114, 116, 141, 219

Q

Queen of Peace (Kern, Charles), 174–191, 235

R

Rainwater, harvesting from roof, 127
Registration, 227
Remote work, 40
Roof, raising, 149–150
Roof decks, 37, 49
RV parks, 229
    sustainability at, 19–20
RVs, 78
    purchase of ready-made, 48

S

Sam's Club, 229
School buses, 8, 18, 24–37, 197
    cost of buying, 18
    engines in, 18
    renovating, from scratch, 18–19
    tips and features of, 26
Shared lifestyles communities, 20–21
Shelving, 28, 35, 171
Shipping container, retrofitting into workshop, 108–109
Showers, 30, 33, 59, 73
Shower-tub, 156
Shuttle buses, 8, 197, 199
    conversion of, 136, 139
Skoolies, 21, 42
    meet-ups for, 42
Skylights, 59
Sleeping alcove, 96–98
Solar power, 8, 26, 40, 42, 54, 57, 159, 165, 225
    rooftop, 49
Sound system, 171
Stairs, 156
State Farm, 227
Storage, 69
    basket, 72
    book, 29
    hidden, 43
    under seat, 57, 99, 166
    underbed, 119, 120
    underfloor, 177, 188
"Stormy," 40, 43

Sullivan, Brian and Starla, bus conversion of, 110–123, 205, 234
"Superior Truck," 15
Sustainability at RV parks, 19

T

Tado, 139–140
Technologies
    battery, 225
    leveraging, 8
    offgrid, 230
Thigpen, Virginia, bus conversion of, 134–145
Thompson, Jeremy and Mira, bus conversion of, 90–109, 234
Tin Can Tourists, 15
Tiny houses, 9–13, 21, 66
    attributes of, 12
    cost of, 9, 12
    as environmentally friendly, 12
    festivals for, 21
    moving, 19
    sizes of, 9
    as symbol of more sustainable lifestyle, 12
    on wheels, 21
Toilets, 30, 33, 42, 67, 73, 86, 102, 117, 127, 156
Trant, Kate, 15
Trapdoors, 177
Trebitowski, Brandon and Ashley, bus conversion of, 52–63, 232, 233
Twitchell, James B., 14, 21

V

Ventilation, 220
Volkman, Kyle, bus conversion of, 160–173, 229, 235

W

Walmart, 229
"Walter" (Davis, Luke and Rachel), 146–159
Waste, 225
    reducing your, 225
Waste vegetable oil (WVO), 20, 127, 162, 165, 200
Water
    black, 165, 225
    fresh, 54, 156, 224–225
    grey, 67, 225
Water heater, 30, 165
Water pump, 26
Water tanks, 30, 79
We Got Schooled (Ayers, Ryan, and Meccio, Justine), 24–37, 223
    tips and features, 26
We Got Schooled (blog), 26
Wheeled trailer bases, 12
Where We Roam (Manning, Emily and Scott), 76–89
    tips and features, 79
Winnebago Nation (Twitchell), 14, 21
Woodstoves, 42, 46, 99, 165, 169, 190, 219–220

Y

Yetibus (Volkman, Kyle), 160–173, 229, 235
    tips and features in, 165

Z

Zoning regulations, 13

Kimberley Mok is a writer, designer, and illustrator whose work focuses on sustainable architecture, design, art, culture, and technology. She has a bachelor's degree in architecture from Cornell University, and she is a certified permaculture designer and yoga teacher. Kimberley is passionate about alternative dwellings and small-space design and has studied, collaborated, and lived in a number of unique structures around the world, from lofty treehouses to rammed earth structures, geodesic domes, zomes, van conversions, tiny houses, micro-apartments, and hurricane-resistant homes. Her work has appeared on the websites TreeHugger, The New Stack, Spacing, Planet Green, Mother Nature Network, AlterNet, Yahoo! Green, and Parentables. Originally from Toronto, Canada, Kimberley now resides near Montreal.